THE SOUTH CAROLINA EDUCATION ASSOCIATION

Terry M. McMillan
President
1987-1988

DEDICATION

   This book has been donated in honor of the founders
of the Palmetto Education Association, whose skill and
dedication exemplify the finest qualities inherent in all
education professionals. These dedicated individuals,
unselfishly, and with great purpose, gave their best to
the children of this State in the hope that the future
growth and progress of South Carolina will set the
example for the rest of the nation to follow.

421 Zimalcrest Drive ● Columbia, SC 29210 ● 803-772-6553
Affiliated with the National Education Association

A HISTORY OF
THE PALMETTO
EDUCATION
ASSOCIATION

A HISTORY OF THE PALMETTO EDUCATION ASSOCIATION

by
John F. Potts, Sr.

National Education Association
Washington, D.C.

Library of Congress Cataloging in Publication Data

Potts, John F., Sr.
    A history of the Palmetto Education Association.
    Includes bibliographical references.

    1. Palmetto Education Association—History.
2. Education—South Carolina—History.
I. NEA Teacher Rights (Organization)   II. Title.
L13.P283P67   370'.6'2757   78-6977

DEDICATION

To the founders and former members of the Palmetto Education Association who did so much with so little for so many. May we always remember their unselfish and devoted services to the teaching profession and to the progress and development of the people of South Carolina.

CONTENTS

Author John F. Potts, Sr.

About the Author

John F. Potts, Sr., president emeritus of Voorhees College in Denmark, South Carolina, has devoted his entire career to the service of education. Starting as an elementary school teacher, he served as high school teacher and elementary and high school principal, and was the president of Voorhees College for 16 years. After his retirement, he became executive director of the Triangle Association of Georgia) and the Moton College Service Bureau. Presently he is serving as a consultant to several colleges in the areas of proposal preparation and evaluation.

Dr. Potts served the Palmetto Education Association as vice-president, as chairman of the Program Committee, and as president from 1946 to 1950. After his tenure as president, he continued to serve as a member of the Executive Committee and chairman of the Department of Higher Education. He was also a member of the joint committee of the Palmetto Education Association and the South Carolina Education Association that made the merger plans for the two organizations.

Among Dr. Potts' other published works are *A History of the Growth of the Negro Population of Gary, Indiana; Black Student Affairs; The Moton Institute Support Services Handbook;* and several articles of educational interest in professional journals.

Acknowledgments

Many people contributed to the preparation of this manuscript to whom the author owes a debt of gratitude. The number is too large to name each one, but there are some who deserve special recognition. Among them are the members of the Palmetto Education Association History Project Committee who gave inspiration, guidance, and many times very significant information which was not in the written record. The members of this committee are Chairperson Alberta T. Grimes, Hudson L. Barksdale, James T. McCain, Dr. J. T. W. Mims, Dr. W. E. Solomon, and Dr. Agnes Wilson.

All of the members of this committee except Dr. Solomon and Dr. Wilson are former presidents of the Palmetto Education Association. Dr. Solomon served as executive secretary of the Palmetto Education Association from 1950 to 1967. Dr. Wilson was elected president of the merged PEA and South Carolina Education Association in 1973. To Dr. Mims the author gives special thanks for providing him with some of the missing *Bulletins* which could not be found in the records.

In addition, Dr. Samuel B. Ethridge, special assistant to the executive director of the National Education Association, deserves a special expression of thanks for his support.

The author is also grateful to Mrs. Ella Clyde Myers Stevens for sending the records of the Association that her father, I. M. A. Myers, executive secretary from 1918 to 1928, had kept over the years. This contribution was very valuable because there were no records of these early years in the Association's files.

The Reverend Stephen C. Campbell, now deceased, gave the author permission to use some of the information contained in his master's degree thesis relating to private secondary education in South Carolina.

Others who provided information were John R. Harper, PEA treasurer for many years; Larrie J. Foster, an active member in both PEA and SCEA; Edward E. Taylor, former president of SCEA and former vice-president of PEA; Mrs. Ellen C. Watson and Dr. Lelia Bradby, both former PEA presidents; and Mrs. Allard Allston, granddaughter of Mrs. J. L. Cain, wife of one of the founders of the PEA.

Miss Barbara J. Williams, head librarian of South Carolina State College, provided along with other materials a copy of *A Tentative History of South Carolina State College* written by Dean N. C. Nix; and James H. Williams, NEA associate director of affiliate relations, sent copies of the merger evaluations for South Carolina for 1969, 1974, and 1975.

Most of the research covering the early period from 1868 to 1930 was done by Paula M. Potts, the research assistant for this project, who earned her master's degree in educational research from the University of South Carolina. Since there was very little information about the Association in the PEA files before 1946, her services were very helpful.

The author is also grateful to Mrs. Blakie Bailey, secretary to Dr. Solomon, for her assistance in making the necessary records available and providing additional information when these data were requested. My gratitude is also extended to my wife, Muriel Logan Potts, for typing the manuscript and for her encouragement and assistance with the research.

To all of those individuals providing assistance whose names I have not mentioned and to those who searched in vain for materials requested by me, I am deeply grateful.

Preface

This written history of the Palmetto Education Association was sponsored jointly by the South Carolina Education Association and the National Education Association. When the American Teachers Association united with the National Education Association in 1966, one of the stipulations of the merger was the publication of the history of the American Teachers Association and the histories of the predominantly black state teachers' associations. When the Palmetto Education Association merged with the South Carolina Education Association in April 1967, the publication of a history was discussed; but no positive action was taken at that time.

In October 1975 this writer was requested by the Palmetto Education Association History Project Committee to write this history. To fulfill the promise from the South Carolina Education Association and the National Education Association that a history of the Palmetto Education Association be written, I accepted the invitation of the Committee.

Preserving for posterity the record of an organization that did so much to raise educational standards and equalize educational opportunities is both challenging and humbling. Nevertheless, this chronicle covers the period from the founding in 1900 to the merger in 1968—a period of 68 years. The epilogue provides a historical background of public education in South Carolina beginning with the Constitutional Convention of 1868 when the public school system was established. The prologue focuses upon what has happened since the merger.

A serious attempt has been made to accurately describe the efforts, achievements, and even the failures of the organization rather than write a series of biographical sketches of the leaders. However, the achievements of the leaders are indirectly recorded as the progress of the Association is described. It is my sincere desire that this effort will meet the expectations of those about whom it is written as well as those for whom it was written.

John F. Potts, Sr.

1868-1900: A Historical Background of Public Education in South Carolina

What's past is prologue.

Shakespeare

The history of an organization usually begins many years before its actual birth. Just as a child is conceived many months before it is born, most organizations have deep roots in the years immediately preceding their date of birth. The Palmetto Education Association was no exception to this pattern. The date of its formal organization was 1900, but its roots extend to the time when the public school system in South Carolina was established by the Constitutional Convention in 1868. The predominantly black delegation, after very serious deliberation, prepared a new state constitution which provided for public education to "all children between the ages of six and sixteen."[1] There were some feeble attempts to establish a statewide system of free public education before 1868, but these efforts were unsuccessful for several reasons: (1) education was considered the responsibility of the church; (2) private academies were established; (3) free schools bore the stigma of being for paupers; and (4) slave insurrection was feared as a result of free public education.

RELIGIOUS AND BENEVOLENT SOCIETIES

Education was considered a private affair that was the responsibility of the church rather than the state. Episcopalians established

15

the first church schools in the colony in the early eighteenth century. A church society organized in London known as the Society for the Propagation of the Gospel in Foreign Parts provided "instruction in religion and morals, in the three R's"[2] and trained the boys for trades and the girls for domestic service.

Other religious denominations entered the educational field, and the cause of education was promoted by other societies incorporated in the state between 1751 and 1809. To a limited extent the schools established by these societies and churches met some of the needs of public education. The principal sources of financial support for these schools were gifts and bequests from individuals and both secular and religious societies.

PRIVATE ACADEMIES

As important as the educational efforts of the churches were, the most commonly accepted plan of education in South Carolina was the establishment of private academies financed by tuition fees. This is supported by Calyer Meriwether in his *History of Higher Education in South Carolina:* "But these free, charity, and religious schools were not the only ones. A large portion of the education was done by private schools and academies."[3] Another account relates the following: "From the time of the founding of the colony up to the 1960's —a period of some two hundred years—the well-to-do in South Carolina patronized private schools or employed tutors for their sons and governesses for their daughters. Prior to the founding of higher institutions of learning, and to some extent, even after that time, the sons of the rich were sent away to be educated—sometimes to northern states, but more often to Europe.[4]

The large number of private academies supported by tuition fees throughout the state was a great obstacle to the establishment of a free school system. As early as 1811, the Honorable Stephen Elliott of Charleston, known as the "father of the first public school system in South Carolina," introduced an act before the state legislature to provide elementary instruction *to all people free of charge.* However, "no arrangement was made for the education of Negro children."[5] This act met bitter and determined opposition from a large influential segment of the people that objected strenuously to increased taxation

16

of any kind and regarded education as the duty of the individual rather than the responsibility of the state.

THE STIGMA ON FREE SCHOOLS

The widespread belief that free schools were for paupers was still another reason for the defeat of these early attempts to inaugurate a free public school system in South Carolina. Meriwether points out that "the favoring of paupers was probably the greatest cause of the failure of the system."[6] The rich did not need public education, and the poor were too proud to send their children to free schools lest they bear the stigma of being poor.

Henry T. Thompson agrees with Meriwether: "It may be false pride which induces a man to attempt to conceal the fact that he is too poor to maintain those dependent upon him, but it is nevertheless true that such is the case in all classes of society. Many men would deprive their children of the means of education in preference to having them branded as paupers."[7]

It appeared that the prevailing opinion in the state was that there was no need for a public education system, and that private instruction could provide all that was needed except that special arrangements (unacceptable as they were) had to be made for the poor.

FEAR OF SLAVE INSURRECTION

Another source of strong opposition to a free public school system in South Carolina was the fear of slave insurrections if slaves were taught to read and write. The early parochial schools provided the slaves some elementary education, but several slave insurrections gave rise to the idea that it was unsafe to impart knowledge to them. Laws were then passed imposing penalties for teaching slaves to read and write. This is an explanation for Elliott not providing for the education of Negroes in the act he introduced in the South Carolina legislature in 1811.

By 1822, after Denmark Vesey led an insurrection in Charleston, the educational progress of Negroes was still suffering serious setbacks. About 1835, the following law was passed:

An act to amend the law relating to Slaves and Free Persons of Color.—Be it enacted by the Honorable, the Senate and House of

17

Representatives now met and sitting in General Assembly and by the authority of the same. If any person shall hereafter teach any slave to read or write, or cause or procure any slave to read or write, such person if a free white person upon conviction thereof shall for each and every offense against this act be fined not exceeding One Hundred Dollars and imprisoned not more than six months; or if a free person of color shall be whipped not exceeding fifty lashes, and fined not exceeding Fifty Dollars, at the discretion of the Court of Magistrates and Freeholders before which such person of color is tried; and if a slave to be whipped at the discretion of the court; not exceeding fifty lashes; the informer to be entitled to one half of the fine and to be a competent witness. And if any free person of color or slave shall keep any school or other place of instruction for teaching any slave or free person of color to read or write, such free person of color or slave shall be liable to the same fine and corporal punishment as are by this act imposed and inflicted upon free persons of color and slaves for teaching slaves to read or write.[8]

CONSTITUTIONAL CONVENTION OF 1868

With such strong opposition to a free public school system coming from the most powerful and influential sources in the state, it is remarkable indeed that delegates to the Constitutional Convention of 1868 were successful in establishing a statewide system of public education for the children of all the citizens of South Carolina. Two very significant circumstances provided the opportunity for this action to be taken.

1. One of the mandates of Reconstruction following the Civil War was the writing of a new constitution acceptable to Congress. This legislation was forced upon South Carolina and other southern states as a condition for rejoining the Union.

2. The delegates elected by counties to this convention did not represent the white power structure. Like most of the constitutional conventions in the South during this period, the delegation was composed of Negroes, northern-born white men who were derisively referred to as "carpetbaggers," and poor white Southerners who were disdainfully called "scalawags." The 76 Negro delegates outnumbered the 48

white delegates by a large margin. This reflects the fact that Negro voters were in the majority in 21 of the state's 31 counties. There were 80,000 Negroes registered to vote in 1867 compared with 46,000 white voters.

Lerone Bennett, Jr., in his book *Before the Mayflower: A History of Black America,* points out that "South Carolina's Constitution, like most Reconstruction Constitutions, made the state a much more positive force in the lives of the people. It eradicated every form of slavery, abolished imprisonment for debt, authorized universal male suffrage and gave the state its first divorce law."[9] He further states that "Black delegates were largely responsible for the most important innovation in Reconstruction governments—the establishment of a public school system for poor and rich, black and white."[10] The proceedings of the Constitutional Convention of 1868 support the observation that black delegates played a very significant role in the enactment of this legislation. Francis L. Cardoza of Charleston, who later was principal of Avery Institute, state secretary and treasurer, served as chairman of the Committee on Education. Another black man, Robert Smalls from Beaufort, offered the following resolution early in the three-month session:

Whereas, the maintenance of an intelligent government faithful to the interests and liberties of the people, must in a great measure depend upon the intelligence of the people themselves; and,

Whereas, the experience of those States which have opened to the poor and rich alike the opportunities of instruction has demonstrated the utility of common schools in elevating the intellectual character of their population; therefore

Resolved, That the Committee on the Constitution be directed to report an article providing for a system of common schools, of different grades, to be open without charge to all classes of persons.

Resolved, That for the purpose of making effective the common school system, it be required that all parents and guardians send their children between the ages of seven and fourteen to some school, at least six months for each year, under penalties for non-compliance, to be fixed by law, unless from sufficient cause any may be excused in writing by some proper legal authority appointed to direct or superintend the public schools.[11]

This resolution was referred to the Committee on Education, and in February (the session lasted from January 14 to March 17, 1868) the Committee made its first report.

It is very similar to Article X which after a third reading was adopted by the Convention and became an integral part of the Constitution. The major differences between the first report of the Committee on Education and the final adopted document was the deletion of the preamble to the first report and the elimination of Sections 9 and 11 in the original document, leaving the final draft with ten rather than twelve sections.

The debates which occurred during the Convention are very revealing. They tell more about the concerns and the desires of the delegates than may be found elsewhere in history. For example, a discussion between A. J. Ransier and F. L. Cardozo was concerned with the use of the words "race" and "color" in the Constitution. Ransier did not think they were necessary, but Cardozo insisted that the language be specific. His answer to Ransier follows:

> It is a potent fact that, as colored men, we have been cheated out of our rights for two centuries, and now that we have the opportunity, I want to fix them in the Constitution in such a way that no lawyer, however cunning or astute, can possibly misinterpret the meaning. If we do not do so, we deserve to be, and will be cheated again. Nearly all the white inhabitants of the state are ready at any moment to deprive us of these rights, and not a loop hole should be left that would permit them to do it constitutionally.[12]

The framers of the Constitution had the necessary foresight to include two very significant provisions in the first public school system. They wanted to be sure that the long-established theory of separation of church and state be maintained in South Carolina. Section 5 of Article X contains this provision:

> No religious sect or sects shall have exclusive right to, or control of any part of the school funds of the State, nor shall sectarian principles be taught in the public schools.[13]

Equally as important was their insistance that the schools for black and white children *not* be separated. Cardozo in defense of this position made the following statement:

> We have not provided that there be separate schools. . . . It is simply left so that if any colored child wishes to go to a white

school, it shall have the privilege to do so. I have no doubt, in most localities, colored people would prefer separate schools, particularly until some of the present prejudice against their race is removed.[14]

Even though Cardozo and those who agreed with his position knew that black parents would most likely at that time send their children to black schools, they did not want to establish a segregated school system.

WHITE OPPOSITION TO FREE PUBLIC SCHOOLS

Henry T. Thompson in his book *The Establishment of the Public School System of South Carolina* gives this account of the reception the white people of South Carolina gave to the adoption of the Constitution of 1868:

> The white people of the State inveighed bitterly against the adoption of the Constitution of 1868—an importation from the North which was grafted upon their legal system for the purpose of enforcing Reconstruction. They pronounced it "the work of Northern adventurers, Southern renegades, and ignorant Negroes." Strange to relate, however, this Constitution remained the law of the State for twenty seven years. Although it was adopted over the indignant protest of the white people, they made no effort to frame another in its stead until eighteen years after their return to power. From this it would seem that the Constitution of 1868 was better adapted to their condition than was at first thought to be the case.[15]

With the bitter opposition to the adoption of the American system of free public schools which the state constitution provided, it is not surprising that there was great difficulty in the implementation of the legislation. The state superintendent elected under the Reconstruction regime was J. K. Jillson, a white man from Massachusetts. He was highly qualified and labored faithfully to put the newly adopted school system into operation. However, the odds were heavily against him. During his eight years of service from 1868 to 1877, he was in the untenable position of having responsibility without authority and increasing indebtedness without the necessary financial support. In addition, Jillson made himself obnoxious to the white people of the state by his insistence upon mixed schools. In a letter he wrote to a superintendent of a state institution, he stated:

21

The following points relative to the admission of colored pupils in this institution will be rigidly and strictly insisted upon: (1) Colored pupils must not only be admitted into the institution on application but an earnest and faithful effort must be made to induce such pupils to apply for admission. (2) Such pupils when admitted must be domiciled in the same building, must eat at the same table, must be taught in the same classrooms, and by the same teachers, and must receive the same attention, care and consideration as white pupils.[16]

POST-RECONSTRUCTION

When the federal troops were withdrawn from the State House in Columbia on April 10, 1877 and the government was returned to the newly elected officials, a new state superintendent, Hugh S. Thompson, took office. He held this position from 1877 to 1882. He, too, encountered some serious obstacles, but they were somewhat different from those experienced by Jillson. Probably the most serious was the added expense required by the separate schools for the two races.

With the end of the Reconstruction in 1877 bringing about the restoration of power to the white people, there was a period of great indifference to public education which at times bordered on actual hostility. The philosophy of the old power structure that education was a private affair and not necessarily conducive to good citizenship prevailed.

Even though Thompson established a segregated school system, he must be given credit for changing the attitude of many influential citizens in the state about the value of free public education during his six-year tenure in office. His first task was persuading the people to raise the necessary funds by taxation. His second task was securing professionally trained teachers.

TEACHER INSTITUTES

At that time there was a lack of appreciation of the value of professional training for teachers. Thompson felt that a teacher should be trained as much as a doctor, a lawyer, a dentist, or a minister. To provide this training he recommended teacher conventions, teacher institutes, and normal schools as agencies which would improve the quality of teaching. The legislature did not immediately provide the funds for the normal schools requested by Superintendent Thompson. He did, however, establish summer teacher institutes. The first one was held in Spartanburg in 1880 at Wofford College with a donation of $1,000 from the Peabody Fund. This first teacher institute was such a remarkable success that a second was held at Furman University in Greenville in 1881. At that time the South Carolina State Teachers Association was organized. During the summer of 1882, a third teacher institute was held in Columbia at South Carolina College.

The earliest Institute for Colored Teachers was held in Charleston in October 1880 under the supervision of Bishop P. F. Stevens, the county school commissioner.[17] This was limited to Charleston County and lasted only a week, but it was a necessary first step in raising the dignity of the profession for black teachers. During the following summer of 1881, "an Institute for Colored Teachers was held in Columbia during the four weeks of July, under the direction of Professor H. P. Montgomery, an able colored teacher of Washington, D.C., assisted by a capable corps of instructors. The Institute opened with a large attendance which steadily increased until the enrollment reached 185. A second successful State Institute for Colored Teachers, again under the management of Professor Montgomery, was held in Columbia during the summer of 1882."[18]

Within a few years after the inauguration of these summer institutes by Superintendent Thompson, normal training schools were founded.

FORMATION OF PROFESSIONAL ORGANIZATIONS

Equally important were the professional organizations which grew out of these summer institutes. Reference has already been made to the organizing of the South Carolina State Teachers Association in 1881. Nineteen years later in, 1900, its black counterpart with the same name (later changed to Palmetto Education Association) was born under very similar circumstances.

A question may be raised about the 19-year span of time between the founding of the two associations. While all of the reasons may not be known, the time difference may be attributed to two major factors: (1) the attitude of the state and county superintendents toward the education of Negroes and (2) the presence of a large number of private schools for Negroes that to some degree compensated for the inadequacies of the public schools.

INFLUENCE OF SUPERINTENDENTS ON THE ORGANIZING OF BLACK EDUCATORS

The attitude toward the education of Negroes reached a high point with the 1877–82 tenure of State Superintendent Hugh S. Thompson but unfortunately suffered a decline in the years that followed.

Dr. Miller F. Whittaker, in an address to the Palmetto State Teachers Association on March 21, 1940, made the following statement about Superintendent Thompson: "As a result of the farsighted and fair administration of a great educator, the people of the state of both races came into the blessings that attend universal education."[19] He referred to a statement Thompson made in one of his annual reports: "With a majority of 200,000 colored population less than 20 years emancipated from chattel slavery the State of South Carolina should have at heart but one supreme problem—to find out the most expeditious method of lifting (at least) an influential minority of this vast body into the range of the New American Civilization offered by the National Government."[20]

Dr. Whittaker also made the following reference to the teacher institutes: "Realizing the need for good teachers Superintendent Thompson began in 1880 the 'teacher's institutes' which was a new departure in education—attracting the attention of educators all over the country. Interestingly, institutes were held for Negro teachers at the same time in Charleston and Columbia. These institutes gave great impetus to education by introducing new methods and new ideas, and out of these institutes were born the Winthrop College of South Carolina and the State College for Negroes then a part of Claflin University."[21]

Apparently most of the superintendents who immediately followed Thompson did not have the same zeal for educating the Negro. Their annual reports do not reveal the kind of concern Thompson had for the "one supreme problem," as he expressed it in his annual report. There is no mention of any professional improvement opportunities for Negroes in the reports of James H. Rice, who served as state superintendent from 1887 to 1890. He makes reference to the

Teachers' State Association (white) which met in Greenville that year and gives this description of the county institutes: "Institutes have been held in several of the counties and the commissioners report a good attendance."[22] Since the reports did not mention any efforts to upgrade the education of Negroes, it is assumed that Mr. Rice did not consider this one of his duties.

When the next state superintendent, W. D. Mayfield, took office in 1891, there was a revival of the county institutes for both white and Negro teachers. However, these institutes were limited to one week. Special attention was given to subject matter, content, and methodology. There were some demonstrations, and many of the lectures were open to the public to increase an interest in education in the communities. The county institutes for colored teachers were, with the exception of Spartanburg County, directed and taught by Negro principals and faculty members from Claflin College. A team of teachers with a director would move from county to county spending a week in each. In Spartanburg a team of white teachers conducted sessions for white teachers from 10 a.m. to 1 p.m., and a separate institute was held for the "colored teachers in the colored school building in the afternoon from 4:00 to 7:00 p.m. . . ."[23] The director of each county institute was required to submit a lengthy report to the state superintendent of education. Unlike the previous superintendent, Mr. Mayfield placed a high priority on the improvement of teacher training programs and made provision for Negro teachers to participate in large numbers. However, his administration from 1881 to 1898 created a control over the education of Negroes by the state superintendent that lasted until the fight for equalization of salaries began many years later. In his *Twenty-third Annual Report,* Mr. Mayfield made this statement: "The holding of Teachers' Institutes should be a positive requirement of law and no longer remain simply permissive. They should be placed under the management and control of the State Superintendent of Education."[24] The State Board of Examiners then met and passed a resolution giving the state superintendent this authority. This control did not provide a climate conducive to independent action and may have been a strong factor in delaying the organization of a teachers' association for Negro teachers.

In 1899, when John J. McMahan was elected superintendent, he discontinued the county institutes and established in their place four-week summer schools. The first year there were forty for white teachers and eight for Negro teachers.[25] At that time there were 3,076 white teachers and 125,000 students enrolled compared with 2,166 black teachers and 150,787 black students.

Superintendent McMahan had a very unfavorable opinion of Negro teachers. In the *Thirty-first Annual Report* he has this to say about them:

> In the rules for granting certificates upon examinations, careful discrimination needs to be made to fit the requirements of white and Negro schools respectively. . . . The degree of preparation of the Negro teachers that are available is the limit to the preparation that the law should require of them. But the material at hand for white teachers is of as much higher grade as the culture and education of the white race is higher.[26]

Here Mr. McMahan is suggesting a double standard of certification because "we must have teachers for the Negro schools."[27]

Not only did Mr. McMahan believe that the Negro teacher was inferior, he also had that same opinion about all Negroes. In the *Thirty-first Annual Report* he makes this statement in his description of how the Negro should be educated: "The argument often advanced that book-learning carries a Negro to the penitentiary may have some element of truth."[28] His obvious position on the education of Negroes was to provide them with manual training but not to prepare them for the professions.

Probably the best example of Mr. McMahan's belief in the inferiority of the Negro was his placing white directors and instructors in charge of the Negro summer schools. In the *Thirty-second Annual Report,* he explains his action this way:

> In order, therefore to obtain what I should know to be reliable information in this work, I saw that the quality of the work of the Negro teachers must be tested—and those unto whose hands the work is to be mainly entrusted must be measured—through the medium of the best educators in the state whose knowledge of white schools and white teachers would afford the necessary standard. I therefore resolved to hold one strong central school for Negro teachers, in the exclusive charge of white instructors such as I have indicated, and to urge all Negro teachers who have any aspirations to be Summer School instructors in the future to attend this school and make their qualifications known to this faculty of experts.[29]

This "central school for Negro teachers" was financed by a grant from the Peabody Fund. The total amount of the grant for teacher institutes was $2,200. However, there was a stipulation that one-half of the money would be spent for institutes for Negro teachers. Here is a classic example of a white superintendent arbitrarily deciding what must be done for Negro teachers without their involvement in the planning, and using funds which had been granted for another type of professional improvement. He admits that the "attendance was not nearly so large as it should have been, owing to the opposition of a certain class of negro preacher politicians who wish negro 'equality' recognized."[30]

This patronizing attitude of Superintendent McMahan is further illustrated by the following statements made in the same reports: "I appreciate as keenly as any man in South Carolina the crime of the Fifteenth Amendment, which has given the South negro suffrage as a menace to the preservation of the white man's government, society and race."[31]

It was first suggested by Mr. McMahan that this summer session be held at "the State Negro School in Orangeburg,"[32] but it was finally decided to use Benedict College instead because it had a white president.

In the report of this summer session to the superintendent made by E. L. Hughes, chairman of the faculty, there is another strong reference to the great need of controlling the kind of education Negroes were to receive. The statement is as follows:

> For myself, I believe that the educational leaders and authorities, who are of the white race, should exercise a controlling influence upon the education of the negroes, for the good of both races. It seems to me that the only vital question regarding negro education which is in the power of the white man to answer is not whether he shall be educated, or how much, but how shall he be educated, and what kind of education shall he receive. To answer that, the white people should not stand aloof but take hold wherever it is possible, and dominate not only the educational machinery which is already done, but shape the educational thought and create the educational atmosphere—these are more important.[33]

This statement is even more significant because the writer, Mr. Hughes, was superintendent of the Greenville graded schools at that time and was expressing the prevailing opinion of the superintendents of the state. He and other superintendents who assisted him in the summer school (W. H. Hand of Chester and Frank Evans of Spartanburg) had acceptable educational credentials, but many of the county superintendents had very inadequate qualifications for their positions, and some of them did not think that taxes of white people should be spent to educate Negroes.

Fred L. Brownlee in his book *New Day Ascending* tells this incident about a county superintendent:

> The experiences of county superintendents vary, but generally reflect a more or less common pattern. At the beginning some of them did not know the location of the Negro schools. They were prone to drift along, avoiding their responsibility whenever possible. A fairly common instance is that of a state agent who, after numerous but futile attempts to draw the attention of a county superintendent to the need for a Negro high school, finally brought the matter to a head by casually dropping in at a meeting of the board of education, even though uninvited. The Chairman let him speak. He seized the opportunity to talk about Negro schools. . . . When he finished, the chairman spoke for the board saying, "We don't mean to build schools for those people."[34]

ROLE OF PRIVATE SCHOOLS FOR NEGROES

The presence of a large number of private schools for Negroes that to some degree compensated for the inadequacies of the public schools was no doubt a contributing factor to the nineteen-year lag in the founding of the two organizations. All of the schools offering any secondary work were privately established by churches, benevolent persons, or outside educational agencies. It is noteworthy to mention that until 1910 the only public high school in South Carolina was Howard School in Columbia. Howard School also has the distinction of being the first public school in the state of South Carolina. It was opened in 1867 with 600 students in attendance the first year. It is surprising to many to learn that a Negro school was the first public school to be established in South Carolina ante-dating the Constitutional Convention of 1868. Even more significantly, it was the only existing public school in the state until 1910. O. B. Martin, state superintendent from 1903 to 1909, recommended that consideration be given to establishing high schools. The result was the enactment of the first high school law of 1907. The schools were not actually in operation until a few years later.

Columbia has the distinction of having the first public school; but Charleston, where private schools were more prevalent even before the Freedman's Bureau was in operation, provided the earliest schools. The best known and the most influential of these schools was Avery Normal Institute organized by F. L. Cardoza on October 1, 1865, two years before Howard School opened. Cardoza was the first principal. Avery was supported by the American Missionary Association of the Congregational Church and was named for a minister who gave a large part of the money for the construction of the school on Bull Street. This school had an outstanding reputation for academic excellence.

Other private schools established in Charleston were Shaw Memorial Institute, named for the famous Colonel Robert G. Shaw, and Wallingford Academy founded by Jonathan G. Gibbs.

Throughout the state, there were numerous other private schools for Negroes. Among them were the following: Penn School on St. Helena Island founded in 1864; Mather School in Camden founded by the Missionary Women of the Methodist Episcopal Church; Laing Normal and Industrial School in Mount Pleasant; and Schofield School in Aiken founded by the Quakers. The Board of Missions of the Presbyterian Church established Brainard Institute in Chester in 1868 and also founded Goodwill School in Sumter County and Maynesville Institute in Mayesville. (Mary McLeod Bethune began her education at Mayesville Institute.) Fairfield Normal Institute at Winnsboro and the Mattoon School in Greenville were both started by the Presbyterian Church. The Reverend Alexander Bettis, a Negro ex-slave, founded Bettis Academy in Trenton, South Carolina in 1881; and Brewer Normal in Greenwood was organized by the Congregational Church in 1872.

The Negro Baptists in South Carolina probably made the greatest contribution to the education of Negroes between 1880 and 1915. The Reverend Stephen C. Campbell, in his master's degree thesis entitled *The Influence of Negro Baptists on Secondary Education in South Carolina,* reminds us that "more than half of the people in the State were Baptists" and "there were more than one thousand Baptist churches."[35] According to the Reverend Mr. Campbell, the churches organized into associations and established associational schools in the Pine Belt and Piedmont sections of the state. There were 21 of these schools supported by funds raised by the associations from collections, tuition, farm products, and gifts. "These schools filled a great need in secondary education and met the needs of the communities where they were located. Though they were small, inadequately supported and poorly equipped, they pointed the way to the need for better school buildings, better teachers and longer terms."[36]

Considering that most of the four-year private colleges for Negroes in the state—Allen University, Benedict College, Claflin College, Morris College, and Voorhees College—had high school departments, it is even more evident that from 1868 to 1916 Negroes had to depend upon private institutions to provide the education they received. Since teachers' associations grew out of the need to improve instruction in public schools, it is not difficult to understand why a state association for Negro teachers was not established earlier. This probably also accounts for the lack of real interest in the association until 1918, which is discussed in Chapter I.

These private four-year colleges for Negroes, including State College, actually continued their high school departments until the 1930's because the highest grade at most public schools was the tenth.

EDUCATIONAL FOUNDATIONS

No account of the Negroes' struggle against ignorance can be complete without referring to the assistance given by educational foundations. The Slater and Jeanes Funds, under the direction of Dr. James H. Dillard, helped to improve education for Negroes in rural areas. The General Education Board aided in acquiring buildings and equipment. The Julius Rosenwald Fund contributed to the erection of public school buildings. This fund also supported libraries for Negro public schools and aided in consolidation.

Without the assistance given by these and other foundations, public education in South Carolina for Negroes would have been even more deplorable than it actually was during this period.

CHAPTER I

1900-1918: Early Attempts to Organize

History is the confluence of two streams—the stream of circumstance and the stream of human effort.

Charles A. Beard and Mary R. Beard

Tracing the history of education in South Carolina makes it quite evident that the Palmetto Education Association may not have come into being without the existence of two significant circumstances. One was the establishment of the public school system in 1868 which eventually created as urgent need for well-trained teachers. The other was the establishment of teacher institutes to elevate teaching to a professional status.

The first teacher institute was held in Spartanburg in 1880 at Wofford College. After the second institute was held a year later at Furman University in Greenville, the South Carolina State Teachers Association was organized. However, these institutes and the organization which followed did not benefit black teachers because the state school system was rigidly segregated. It became increasingly clear to black teachers that they had to put forth special efforts to improve their own condition. It was this burning desire on the part of the black teachers in South Carolina to lift themselves by their own bootstraps that brought about the birth of the Palmetto Education Association, known at that time as the South Carolina State Teachers Association.

As was pointed out in the Prologue, the first summer institute for "colored teachers" was held in Columbia in 1881. It is noteworthy that the instructors and the director were from Washington, D.C. and states outside South Carolina. The director, H. P. Montgomery, also conducted another successful institute in 1882. He was one of the supervisors of colored schools in Washington, D.C. and also directed similar institutes for teachers in Virginia.

These two teacher institutes, the county institutes, and the summer sessions provided the impetus for organizing the South Carolina State Teachers Association.

THE STRUGGLE FOR EQUAL OPPORTUNITIES

It is important to observe that the history of this organization reflects the progress or lack of it which the state was expected to make toward the establishment of a public school system designed for *all* of the children of *all* of the people. The lack of equal educational opportunities caused the organization to get a late start. Its counterpart in Alabama started in 1882, and the Virginia Teachers Association began in 1887. The difficulty in determining the exact date of its birth and its slow growth prior to 1918 are also indications of an unfavorable racial climate for the new organization. The reports of state superintendents from Hugh Thompson to J. E. Swearengen over a period of 45 years reveal incredible inequities in funds spent for the education of Negroes. Even as late as 1924 when the reports included more information about Negro education, the comparison of funds spent on Negro children compared to white children reveal wide unequal distribution. *The Fifty-sixth Annual Report of the State Superintendent of Education* indicates that in 1923–24 only $1,400,150 were expended for Negroes as compared with $11,561,849 for white children.[1] At that time the school population was about equal.

Hence it becomes increasingly clear that historically the Palmetto Education Association gained more strength as educational opportunities for Negroes were extended.

It became equally evident to Negro educators and friends of Negro education that Negroes themselves needed to put forth special efforts to improve their training and upgrade the quality of education their pupils were receiving. Paramount in their minds, too, was a more equitable share of the funds which were being spent for public education.

32

Charles and Mary Beard in their monumental work *The Rise of American Civilization* give this definition of history: "History is the confluence of two streams—the stream of circumstance and the stream of human effort."[2] The history of the Palmetto Education Association followed this pattern very closely. Reference has already been made to the circumstances of the times and the human efforts expended by the leaders in education that brought into existence this professional organization.

EARLY YEARS OF ORGANIZATION

Information about this period from 1900 to 1918 is very difficult to find. The *Bulletin* was not published until 1920, and there was no executive secretary until 1918. Either no records were kept about this period; or if they were, they were lost.

The most authentic statement about the founding of the Palmetto Education Association is found in the *Souvenir Program* of the Annual Meeting in March 1948. The first paragraph is as follows:

> The Palmetto State Teachers Association has had a long and rugged existence. The exact date of its organization is not known, nevertheless, it was in the year 1900 that a group of educational leaders of the state, stimulated by the Superintendent of Schools of Richland County and some other teachers working in a Summer Institute at Benedict College, banded themselves together as a State Association. From its beginning until 1918 it operated under the name South Carolina State Teachers Association, and although for eighteen years representatives from only a few counties attended the annual meetings, yet invitations were sent yearly either to all organized county associations or to influential educators in counties where there were no county associations to attend the regular meetings.[3]

It is significant that the state superintendent's reports between 1881 and 1923 have frequent references to the white state teachers' association and no reference to the need for a professional organization for Negroes. John J. McMahan was superintendent when the Association was organized, and his reports from 1900 to 1903 contained no mention of its founding. This is also true of the reports of Superintendent O. B. Martin who served from 1903 to 1907 and Superintendent Swearengen who held the position from 1909 until 1923. The first reference to "the State Teachers Association for colored" was made by in 1923 J. B. Felton, state agent for Negro schools, during the first year of Superintendent Hope's administration.

Equally significant is the fact that the Negro organization came into existence the same year that Superintendent McMahan placed a white director and white teachers in charge of the Negro summer sessions because he felt that there were no Negro educators qualified to teach the Negro teachers. He also stated that there was some opposition to this action from some Negroes who believed in "equality."

In the absence of supportive data from the Palmetto Education Association, we must rely on the very limited information contained in the superintendent's reports. The following impressions are obtained from what was *not* said as well as what was reported: (1) Both state and county superintendents did not encourage a Negro teacher association because they wanted to maintain complete control not only of the financing of Negro education but also the kind and amount of education Negroes should receive; (2) Negro teachers were not qualified but must be certified because Negro teachers were needed to teach Negro children; and (3) Negro principals and college presidents were not qualified to conduct the teacher training programs for Negroes.

These impressions, which are documented in the Prologue, also support the theory of some observers that the Negro teachers' association grew out of the desire of some Negro leaders to free themselves from the domination of the white power structure and organize an association of their own. The summer session being under the complete direction and operation of white superintendents probably precipitated this action. The Association's slow growth between 1900 and 1918 may have been due to intimidation very similar to the pressure put on Negro teachers in later years to prevent them from joining the National Association for the Advancement of Colored People (NAACP).

LEADERSHIP DURING
THE DEVELOPMENTAL YEARS

Some of the leaders who recognized the need for the organization were J. Edward Wallace, principal of Howard High School in Columbia and the first president of the Association; Dr. Thomas Miller, president of State Agricultural and Mechanical College and second Association president; and J. L. Cain, principal of Mayo Graded School in Darlington and the fifth president. Since these three names appear first in the early years of the Association, it is safe to assume that they were among the five founders of the organization. In the tribute to Mr. Cain in the *Bulletin* of April 1944, the following statement appears: "He was one of the five educators who organized the first Negro State Teachers Association."[4] The limited information about this period does not specifically indicate who the other two founders were. However, it is reasonable to assume that they were Nathaniel J. Frederick, the third president of the Association from 1906 to 1908, who later left the teaching profession to enter a legal career and Dr. Robert Shaw Wilkinson, the fourth president, who at that time was on the faculty of the Colored Normal, Industrial, Agricultural, and Mechanical College (South Carolina State) in Orangeburg.

J. EDWARD WALLACE

It is quite interesting to note that the principal of the first public school in South Carolina and for many years the only high school in the state was the first president of the organization. It is unfortunate that there is so little information about Mr. Wallace in the records of the Columbia public school system, at South Carolina State College, or Bennett and Claflin Colleges. Reports of the meetings of the Columbia School Board from 1883 to 1957 contain the following references to him:

> April 18, 1894—Principal Wallace of the Howard School was arrested for resisting an officer. He refused to allow a constable to arrest some children thought to be pupils of Howard School in the school house. The Board received the report as information and notified the Solicitor to notify the constables that they "serve warrants upon the children charged with a crime outside the schoolhouse and in such a manner as not to disturb or interrupt the school."[5]

This item taken from this report has no connection with the history of the organization, but it does tell us something about the first president of the Association. He was fearless enough to resist arrest to protect the rights of the Howard pupils. His action took unusual courage with the double standard of justice that prevailed in 1894.

This incident also indicates that he must have been highly respected by the Columbia Board of Education because they reprimanded the constable rather than the principal. The record points out that on June 26, 1894, the "Case against Principal Wallace nol prossed by the solicitor."[6]

November 20, 1890—Principal J. E. Wallace of Howard School wrote the Board that he had been offered a position elsewhere at a higher salary and on account of his family would have to accept it unless his salary was raised. A motion to raise him $10.00 a month was made, but the votes were two for and two against—motion failed.[7]

November 24, 1890—A motion to raise the Howard principal's salary $10.00 for the last six months of the current school year carried 3 to 1.[8]

October 25, 1899—J. E. Wallace, principal of Howard School resigned to take a chair at the State College for Negroes to which he had been elected.[9]

These items from the reports also provide additional information about Mr. Wallace. They reveal that (1) he must have been highly qualified to be sought by institutions of higher learning; (2) he was not reluctant to ask for a raise—at that time many Negro educators did not have that much nerve; and (3) he was at South Carolina State College, not Howard School, when he was elected president of the Association.

Dean N. C. Nix provides some additional information about Mr. Wallace in *A Tentative History of South Carolina State College.* According to Dean Nix, Mr. Wallace was elected by the trustees of the college to succeed William R. Palmer who resigned in 1899. This action was taken on September 21, 1899. He was appointed to "the Chair of English, Literature and Pedagogics."[10] However, he resigned from this position on September 17, 1903 to accept a position as professor of English and dean of the Normal Department at Claflin College.

The following report obtained from Bennett College gives some additional information about Mr. Wallace's qualification as an educator:

Professor J. E. Wallace, the new president of Bennett College, Greensboro, North Carolina was born in Toronto, Canada, October

21, 1858. He finished the course in the public schools of Toronto and entered the college course at South Carolina University, Columbia, South Carolina, continuing in this college until the junior year, when the institution was closed to colored students, after which he finished his A. B. course in Claflin University, Orangeburg, South Carolina. He served as Chief Clerk in the office of the United States District Attorney in South Carolina from 1881 to 1885, taught school in that state and was principal of Howard High School, Columbia from 1886 to 1900, after which he became Professor of English and Pedagogy at State College for Colored in Orangeburg. Since 1903 he has been Professor of English at Claflin College and Dean of the Normal Department.[11]

The administration of Mr. Wallace as president of Bennett College was brief, lasting from 1913 to 1915. However, the college made significant progress under his leadership. He served as president of the South Carolina State Teachers Association for four years from 1900 to 1904.

DR. THOMAS MILLER

Another founder and second president of the Association from 1904 to 1906 was Dr. Thomas Miller, who was also the first president of South Carolina State College. Like Mr. Wallace, the records of meetings and the actions taken during his two-year administration are not available. However, the history of the college written by Dean Nix contains this description of his training and experiences:

President Miller graduated from Lincoln University [Pennsylvania] in 1872; the same year he served as School Commissioner of Beaufort County; in 1873–74 he studied law at the University of South Carolina and was admitted to the bar in 1875; in 1876–79 he served in the House of Representative of South Carolina; he was elected to the United States Congress September 24, 1890 and served to March 3, 1891; he was returned to the House of Representatives of South Carolina in 1894; and in 1895 he was elected to the State Constitutional Convention.[12]

He was considered a very capable administrator. He served as president of South Carolina State College from 1896 to 1911. During this 15-year period the institution made remarkable progress. Since the teacher institutes and the state teacher summer schools were held at the college, it may be assumed that President Miller's greatest contribution to the South Carolina State Teachers Association was in the area of teacher education.

DR. ROBERT SHAW WILKINSON

The fourth president of the early organization was Dr. Robert Shaw Wilkinson, who served from 1908 to 1914. When he became the Association's president, he was on the faculty of the Colored Normal, Industrial, Agricultural, and Mechanical College (South Carolina State) in Orangeburg. Three years later he assumed his duties as president of South Carolina State College. A biographical sketch includes the following information:

> . . . born at Charleston, South Carolina, February 18, 1865. He received his early training in Shaw Memorial School and Avery Institute of Charleston, South Carolina. He was appointed by Congressman Miller to West Point in 1884, and won first place in the competitive examination. On account of insufficient physical strength he resigned the position in 1885. Accordingly, he entered Oberlin and graduated in the year 1891 as the valedictorian of his class. After graduation, Robert Shaw Wilkinson accepted a position as Instructor at Kentucky State University. On June 28th 1898 he was elected to serve on the first Faculty of the Colored Normal, Industrial, Agricultural and Mechanical College of South Carolina.[18]

J. L. CAIN

The founder who exerted the greatest influence upon the young organization was J. L. Cain, who was appointed principal of Mayo Graded School in Darlington in 1900. Not only was he instrumental in organizing the Association, he has the distinction of having served as the president longer than any other person. His tenure of office was from 1914 to 1922, a period of eight years. Even more significantly, it was during his administration that the Association was completely reorganized, and the membership increased by five times its previous number. A more detailed description of this period will be given in the next chapter.

In the April 1944 issue of the *Bulletin* this tribute was paid to him:

> Professor Cain's ability and efficiency as an educator has received statewide recognition. He was one of the five educators who orga-

nized the Negro State Teacher's Association. . . . He was thrice elected President of this Association and it grew strong rapidly in membership and influence under his leadership. Although he was a young educator, he was constantly in demand as Director of Summer Schools. He served as Director of Summer Schools in Marlboro, Darlington, Horry, Chesterfield, York, Kershaw, Richland, Anderson, Orangeburg and Williamsburg Counties. He organized and built the Upper Pee Dee District Summer School which continued to grow in efficient work and influence until the State College Pee Dee Extension Summer School was established in 1942. He was the first Negro Director of a State Summer School for Negro teachers in South Carolina which was held at Benedict College, Columbia, South Carolina in 1905. He served as Executive Committeeman of the Palmetto State Teachers Association until his health failed and in recognition of his service he was elected Life Member of this Committee.[14]

Mr. Cain built Mayo Graded School from a five-teacher school with an enrollment of 275 to a twenty-four-teacher school with an enrollment of 1,500. It eventually became one of three Negro high schools to receive the first Class 1A rating by the state Department of Education. The other two schools were Booker T. Washington High School in Columbia and Sims High School of Union. His reputation as an outstanding educator became so well known that he was referred to as the "Dean of the Teaching Profession" in South Carolina. He was the youngest of the founders and was active in the affairs of the Association for 43 years. His widow, Mrs. J. L. Cain, served as recording secretary of the Annual Convention until 1954—ten years after his death. The influence of these two dedicated teachers upon the Palmetto Education Association extended over a period of more than five decades.

In addition to the five founders, the March 1948 *Souvenir Program of the Palmetto State Teachers Association* indicates that "some other teachers working in a Summer Institute at Benedict College banded themselves together as a State Association."[15] The *Program* further states that they were "stimulated" by the Richland County Superintendent of Education E. B. Wallace. Although the "other teachers" were not identified, it may be assumed that they were some of those Negro teachers approved by the all-white faculty of that particular summer institute to teach in Negro schools.

39

Dr. Thomas Miller, president of the South Carolina State Teachers Association, 1904-06.

Attorney Nathaniel J. Frederick, president of the South Carolina State Teachers Association, 1906-08.

Dr. Robert Shaw Wilkinson, president of the South Carolina State Teachers Association, 1908-14.

J. L. Cain, principal of Mayo Graded School in Darlington, 1900-1944, and Association president, 1914-22.

CHAPTER II

1918-1940: A Strong Organization Emerges

Education is the fine net which democracy uses in fishing for human talent.

H. G. Wells

The year of 1918 may well be called the "Year of Great Decisions" for the fledgling organization. Indeed, it was the most significant year in the entire history of the Association. Some of the most important decisions made by the leaders were the following:

1. A constitution was formulated and put into operation the following year. This new organizational structure completely changed the work of the Association.

2. An executive secretary was employed to administer the affairs of the organization.

3. Provision was made for the issuance of an annual bulletin.

4. The name was changed to the Palmetto State Teachers Association.

5. The place of the annual meetings was moved from Orangeburg to other cities in the state.

If the organization had a constitution from 1900 to 1918, it has been lost to posterity. As one reads the very limited information available about this period, it becomes apparent that the organization had no real operational structure before 1918. It was very loosely organized and associated with the Orangeburg summer sessions. The teachers seemed to have the impression that the organization had no identity of its own. There was also reluctance on the part of those teachers in some counties to join the Association because of the opposition of the local trustees and county superintendents to the organization.

The history of the Palmetto State Teachers Association which appeared in the *Souvenir Program of the Annual Meeting* in March 1948 provides this information about the early years:

> Very little interest was manifested in the affairs of the Association by the majority of teachers in the State prior to and during the early years of the administration of Professor Cain. The annual meetings were held each year at the State College in Orangeburg during summer sessions; there were but a few persons who attended, and those who attended were largely summer school students who did not attend regularly due to the fact that they did not attend summer school each year. This condition continued year after year, and in 1918 Dr. Wilkinson suggested that the place of meeting of the association be moved to another city so that the teachers might not get the idea that the association was a part of the State College summer session.[1]

It was very evident to the leaders of the organization that drastic action was needed to keep the Association alive. Consequently, they proceeded to engage in a complete reorganization of the body. Even though J. L. Cain had been president since 1914, he remained in that position through the period of reorganization until 1922. This was fortunate for the Association because it needed time to grow and expand under the new constitution before changing leadership. Mr. Cain had the able assistance of the organization's first executive secretary, I. M. A. Myers, who also served as principal of Howard High School in Columbia.

Mr. Myers was not only an efficient administrator but also a good public relations man. He had close contact with the local newspapers as well as the Negro press and wrote numerous articles about the Association and Negro education in general which were published in these papers. Over the years he kept a scrapbook of these clippings which provided valuable information for this history of the Palmetto Education Association. Equally as helpful were the issues of the *Bulletin* dating from 1920 to 1929 that he had assembled and preserved for posterity. Mr. Myers served from 1918 to 1928 and was a very important figure in the Association during the early days of its struggle and helped it gain strength as the years passed.

A NEW NAME: THE PALMETTO STATE TEACHERS ASSOCIATION

It appears that there were some differences of opinion among the leaders of the Association at that time about which person had suggested the change in the name of the organization. The "History" in the *Souvenir Program* of March 1948 indicates that Mr. Myers suggested that the name be changed to the Palmetto State Teachers Association.[2] In *A History of the Palmetto Education Association,* author Guerney Nelson states that Mrs. M. Alice La Saine, longtime Jeanes Supervisor in Charleston County and treasurer of the Association, suggested the new name. According to this source, Mrs. La Saine brought a palmetto tree from Charleston; and, using this tree as a symbol, she urged that the name be changed to the Palmetto State Teachers Association.[3] It is really not too important to find out who gets the credit for changing the name. What is significant is that the membership wanted a name that distinguished the Association from the white teachers organization. Pride in strengthening the organization took precedence over who named it. This change in the name

Mrs. M. Alice La Saine, Jeanes supervisor of Charleston County, PSTA treasurer, 1935-40, and one of those credited with suggesting a new name for the Association.

43

did provide the psychological shot in the arm that the Association needed.

REORGANIZATION

The following statement about the new life the Association was experiencing appeared in the "History and Objectives" included in the *Souvenir Program* of the March 1948 Annual Meeting:

> In 1919 the organization held its annual meeting in Columbia under its reorganized status. More than five times as many persons were in attendance that year as had attended any previous meeting. This increased attendance was due, no doubt, to the increased impetus which was placed upon the membership in the association after its reorganization and to the improved financial status of all people during the war period. In the meeting of 1919 a set of objectives was stated and definite plans were made for the perpetuation of the association. It was thought at this time that the meetings of the association might be held in various cities of the state so that no group of teachers might have an advantage of another group in attending the gatherings from year to year. In the course of years the association has met at Greenville and Spartanburg, but in 1928 it was decided that because of the central location of Columbia and the accessibility of transportation to this point that all future meetings be held in the Capital City.[4]

The earliest record of a constitution is found in the 1922 *Bulletin* of the Association.[5] This document was written in 1918 and revised slightly in 1923. The revised version contained 15 articles, and the by-laws had five sections. The Association operated under this constitution and by-laws until 1939. These purposes were listed:

1. To improve its members in the science and art of teaching.

2. To dignify and promote public interest in the cause of education.

3. To elevate the standards of the teaching profession and improve the Negro race educationally.

Any person actively engaged in any branch of education in the state of South Carolina was eligible for membership by paying dues of $1 per year.

The officers consisted of a president, two vice-presidents, a recording secretary, the executive secretary, a treasurer and an Executive Committee of 10 members elected by ballot. Decision-making power resided in the Executive Committee which also included the president, executive secretary, treasurer, and recording secretary as ex-officio members.

One of the strongest features of this constitution was the provision for an Advisory Council consisting of all the presidents of each county association, who were by virtue of their office also vice-presidents of the state association. This stimulated statewide participation. Another very strong feature was the following provision concerning dues:

> Where all the teachers in the county become members of the State Association and their dues are paid by or prior to February 1st of each year, twenty five percent of said dues may be retained by the Treasurer of the County Association and seventy five percent shall be remitted to the Treasurer of the State Association on or before February 1st of each year.[6]

The by-laws provided for 11 departments for the following groups of teachers: primary, grammar grade, colleges and secondary schools, principals and supervisors, teachers of english, science and mathematics, language, history, education, vocational education, and home economics. The framers of this first constitution provided enough departments to serve the special interests of most of the teachers in South Carolina at that time.

Creating the Advisory Council to get representation for each county, sharing the dues with the counties having 100 percent membership, and appealing to the special interests by the formation of departments were very important factors in the growth of the organization after 1919. More than five times as many teachers joined in 1919 under the reorganized status as had attended any previous meeting.

ANNUAL MEETING, 1920

In the first *Bulletin* published by the Association in 1920, the Reverend I. E. Lowery made this observation:

> The Colored Teachers Association of South Carolina met on March 18th in Coppin Hall at Allen University and continued in session

until Saturday noon. The morning sessions were held at Allen and the afternoon and night sessions were held in the chapel of Benedict College. It is said that 500 teachers attended the Convention. They came from nearly every county in the state. It was an important gathering of Negro educators.[7]

The financial report for 1920 revealed that $393 was collected in registration fees. However, it is quite possible that the attendance reached the 500 figure mentioned by Mr. Lowery because it was not necessary to be a member to attend the general sessions. Of the state's 46 counties, 37 were represented, ranging from one person each from Chester and Greenwood Countys to 75 from Richland County. The second largest number came from Darlington County, the home of the president, J. L. Cain. It is noteworthy that on the college level South Carolina State College was the strongest supporter of the young organization. There were 25 members of that faculty holding membership in 1920, more than the combined number of all of the other institutions of higher learning.

The program of the Annual Meeting held March 18–20, 1920 was the first one to be published in the *Bulletin*. Provision was made in the constitution for the issuance of a bulletin as early as 1918. However, the first publication did not actually appear until 1920. Since this was the first published program, its contents will be described in detail since it set the stage for the programs which followed.

There were four general sessions beginning on Thursday night with the president's address. Another general session was held at 10:30 Friday morning featuring an address by the Honorable J. E. Swearengen, state superintendent of education. There was a Friday afternoon general session at 3:15 when W. H. Hand, superintendent of the Columbia city schools, addressed the teachers and another session on Friday night when President N. B. Young of Florida Normal and Industrial College in Tallahassee, Florida delivered the keynote address. Group meetings were held on Friday morning from 9:00 to 10:30 and Saturday morning from 9:30 to 11:00. At 11:00 on Saturday morning, A. D. Seay, superintendent of education of Richland County, spoke to the membership. According to the Reverend Mr. Lowery, the most enthusiastically received address was delivered by Dr. J. H. Dillard, president of the Jeanes and Slater Funds, who spoke at the general session on Friday morning after the state superintendent. Mr. Lowery said that when Dr. Dillard closed his address "the audience arose en masse and there was an enthusiastic outburst of emotion and of waving of handkerchiefs."[8]

In 1920, President J. L. Cain appointed a School Campaign Committee and described their duties as follows:

. This committee will make a tour of the State, make inquiries about school conditions, study the question of education from every angle and furnish the Bureau with facts collected to be compiled and published as soon as funds are available. This committee hopes to be in a position to furnish the County Superintendents and State Department of Education any information desired pertaining to Negro schools.[9]

The Committee was composed of the president, Mr. Cain; I. M. A. Myers, executive secretary; R. S. Wilkerson, president of State College; R. W. Mance, president of Allen University; B. F. Cox, principal of Avery Institute; S. L. Finley, principal of Finley High School; and Mrs. F. B. Gordon.

The appointment of this committee was significant for two reasons: (1) It was a way of informing the superintendents and the state Department of Education that the Palmetto State Teachers Association expected to be the voice of the Negro teachers. In the future the facts and figures about the education of Negroes were to come from the Negro professional organization. (2) The study conducted by the committee would expose the tremendous inequities in the state's program for the education of white and Negro children.

The following recommendations for the improvement of Negro education were made by the president during this Annual Meeting:

That the upper grades be eliminated from our weakest rural schools so as to enable the primary and intermediate work to be more thoroughly done, these upper grades to be restored as the schools develop in teaching force and other aids.

That the public begin to establish high schools or training schools at each county seat and large population centers to which upper grade pupils from the weak schools may be sent and in which teachers may be trained to help supply the sad need of stronger teachers for colored schools.

That the sub high school grades be gradually eliminated from our colleges so as to enable them to center their efforts upon the better training of the leaders of the race.

That salaries be paid according to preparation, length of service and efficiency to encourage the stronger people to come and to remain in the public school work.[10]

HIGH STANDARDS AND GOALS

These recommendations provide ample evidence of the high calibre of the leaders of the Palmetto State Teachers Association during this reorganization period. One of their paramount objectives was to raise the qualification of teachers and at the same time use every possible means at their command to obtain more adequate compensation for them. Dr. R. S. Wilkinson, president of State College and a member of the Executive Committee, made the following appeal to teachers during the 1921 Annual Meeting held in Columbia:

> As everyone knows, there is a shortage of teachers that is working injury to the children of our state and country that one cannot compute. The number of normal school students is smaller than it was three years ago; the high- and county-training school departments are depleted; and plans to increase them have been discontinued. Other callings that have offered larger compensation have drawn off the teachers until it has come about that a number of schools have been compelled to discontinue their work, and hundreds of persons are working on permits temporarily instead of regular certificates required by the State Department of Education.

> It is not difficult to see the causes of this unfortunate condition, and our people are coming to see it. Theoretically, the people have set teaching high among the callings, but practically they have degraded it by refusing to give teachers a living salary. They are now beginning to realize the critical danger to society of the present situation, and are ready to bid against other callings for the services of other men and women in the public schools. With higher salaries, however, will go the greater consideration and responsibility of those receiving them. Men and women who are now in the profession as well as those who are looking forward to active careers as teachers must qualify to meet these higher demands.[11]

Dr. Wilkinson also made this significant statement in his address: "The time is coming when special preparation will be required of all teachers."[12]

This same emphasis upon raising standards for teachers was stated another way by President Cain in his address to the teachers in March

1922. He referred to the Negro teacher as a "Jack-of-all-trades. He teaches, 'tis true, but he also farms, preaches, laws, barbers, insures, clerks, typewrites, keeps books, sews, cooks, nurses, launders, dresses hair and God only knows what else, in order to eke out an existence."[13] To improve this situation he urged teachers to specialize in teaching and then organize to help themselves improve their financial status:

> The teachers of Negroes should not only be encouraged to specialize, but they should also be persuaded to organize. For one of the most useful lessons that we are called upon to teach our race is the indispensable one of group effort. Unless Negroes learn cooperation they cannot respond to the demands of their age.[14]

This statement by Mr. Cain gives further evidence of the strength of the leadership the Association had during the early twenties when the white power structure took a dim view of Negro organizations. Apparently he was aware of this because he also referred to the wide disparity between the two races in educational opportunities and the fear the white people had of the organization. In this same address he made the following statement:

> There is a very serious duty awaiting the larger development of our association. It is the duty it owes to the whites as well as to the blacks of keeping before both the unwisdom of the present wide disparity in the opportunities of the two races for education . . . one thing feared is our superior numbers. Many whites believe that with an equal education we might become strong enough to overturn their civilization.[15]

During the early twenties there was a gradual increase in membership in the Association. Beginning in 1920, when the first records were available, the membership grew from 393 to 432 in 1921. In 1922 the membership increased to 592, and in 1923 to 659. The counties with the largest number of teachers enrolled during this period were Richland, Darlington, Spartanburg, Marion, and Anderson. Spartanburg's membership increased from 18 to 72 when the annual convention was held there in 1922.

Beginning in 1923 a teachers' directory was published in each *Bulletin*. This was a wise decision for two reasons: (1) teachers were more inclined to join when they saw their names printed in the bulletin and (2) percentages were easier to work out when the exact number of Negro teachers in each county was known. The constitution provided that prizes be given to the three counties with the highest percentage of teachers enrolled.

JOINT COMMITTEE ON ACCREDITED COLLEGES AND HIGH SCHOOLS, 1923

The 1923 *Bulletin* also contained a report of the Joint Committee on Accredited Colleges and High Schools called by State Superintendent J. E. Swearengen on March 23, 1922. The purpose of this conference "was to secure the cooperation of colored representatives of colleges and high schools in order to formulate constructive standard courses of study which should be progressive and suited to the institutions under their control."[16]

It is difficult if not impossible to determine what actually motivated Mr. Swearengen to invite "colored representatives of colleges and high schools" to this conference. Was he really trying to involve the leaders of the new organization in a program of self-improvement or was he finding an excuse for a separate set of standards for Negro schools and colleges? The last part of the statement of purpose— "suited to the institutions under their control"—gives the impression that these standards were applicable to Negro institutions only and that they were less demanding. However, even if this was his main purpose it is gratifying to know that a state superintendent had enough respect and esteem for the Negro educators to have them formulate their standards and devise their own curriculums. This is the first step toward professionalism. No organization can be truly a profession without formulating its own criteria, implementing its programs, and disciplining its members. For the Association to have this opportunity to be involved in an examination of the courses of study in their member institutions and make recommendations for their improvement was a giant step in the right direction. Even if the conference was not called in the name of the organization, it had practically the same effect because all of the committee members were either officers of the Association or members of its Executive Committee.

Representing the colleges were President R. S. Wilkinson, State College, Orangeburg; President R. W. Mance, Allen University, Columbia; President J. J. Starks, Morris College, Sumter; and President C. M. Young, Harbison Institute, Irmo.

The high school representatives were C. A. Johnson, principal of Booker T. Washington High School in Columbia; C. A. Lawson, principal of Lincoln High School in Sumter; and J. L. Cain, principal of Mayo High School in Darlington.

Other educators invited by the chairman to attend the meeting of the Joint Committee at Lincoln High School on April 1, 1922 were as follows: E. R. Roberts, president of Voorhees Institute; J. T. Williamson, State College; R. W. Boulware, Harbison Institute; D. H. Sims, Allen University; D. W. Price, Morris College; Miss M. J. Fitzgerald, Lincoln High School; and Miss V. E. Jacobs, Lincoln High School.

This Joint Committee not only prepared a curriculum for first, second, third, and fourth years in high school but also submitted a curriculum for the Normal Teacher Training Programs. In addition, it submitted 11 recommendations regarding number of teachers required, laboratory requirements, library, budgets, teacher qualifications, equipment, credits, length of recitation periods, and salaries. The minimum salary requested for the year 1922–23 was $750.[17]

PSTA AND STATE SUPERINTENDENTS

In each *Bulletin* of the Association during the decade of the twenties, one significant thing stands out in bold relief—the presidents and other leaders cultivated the goodwill of the state superintendent of education; but at the same time they continuously and persistently kept the needs of Negro administrators, teachers, and pupils before the state officials. They did not hesitate to invite the state and county superintendents and the state agent for Negro schools to participate in their annual conventions, and they kept in close touch with them throughout the year to appraise them of the plight of Negro education.

Reference has already been made to the addresses of J. L. Cain who served as president from 1914 to 1922. His successor was Dr. R. W. Mance, president of Allen University, who stressed the same theme. In the president's address that he delivered in March 1923, he pointed out that 3,575 Negro teachers were employed to teach 243,744 Negro pupils while 7,329 white teachers were hired to teach 235,535 white pupils. More than twice as many white teachers were paid to teach 8,000 fewer children than the Negro teachers instructed. He further pointed out that the per capita expenditure of

51

each white pupil was $36.10 compared to $4.17 for each Negro pupil. The total expenditures for operation of white schools were $5,584,159 compared with $818,248 for Negro schools.[18]

J. P. Burgess, who later became executive secretary in 1928, drafted a resolution in the 1923 convention entitled "The Overloading of Colored Schools." Portions of the resolution follow:

> The observation of teachers here assembled is that in our schools of short terms and overcrowded conditions, entirely too much work is undertaken. We, therefore, wish to go on record as favoring the presenting of a request to the various county superintendents setting forth our observations and suggesting that they call together the various city superintendents, the supervisors of colored schools (where there is one) and some of the most experienced white and colored school men of their respective counties for the purpose of formulating plans for removing this serious handicap.

> Many of our schools have terms of less than four months in length and in some of them the teacher's salary is not more than twenty-five dollars per month.[19]

At this same convention in 1923, the Association appointed a committee to prepare a statement to be presented to Dr. John H. Hope who became the state superintendent in 1923.

This communication to Dr. Hope made a strong and urgent plea for longer terms, larger facilities, better teachers, higher standards, and summer schools for teachers, also pledging the full cooperation

Dr. R. W. Mance, Sr., president of Allen University and PSTA president, 1922-24.

and support of the Colored Teacher's Association of South Carolina in helping him provide better educational opportunities for all.

This persistence continued under the administration of C. A. Lawson, who became president in 1926 and served through 1928. He recommended that county study centers be established in every county and requested the cooperation of the county superintendents in assisting the Association in this effort. Another of Mr. Lawson's recommendations was the centralization of the summer school work for Negro teachers. He requested the Association to prepare a resolution to this effect and submit it to the state Board of Education.

During Mr. Lawson's administration the Association unanimously elected C. A. Johnson, vice-president of the Palmetto State Teachers Association, to represent the South Carolina organization at the convention of the National Association of Teachers in Colored Schools that was held in Durham, North Carolina. In his report Mr. Johnson stated that the Palmetto State Teachers Association "has been a potent factor in arousing our people. This Association is recognized as the spokesman for the Negro teachers of South Carolina."[20] Commenting on the need for higher standards for Negro high schools, Mr. Johnson had this to say:

> A committee from the high school section of our State Teachers Association conferred with the High School Inspector with the view of having our schools standardized. We asked that we be rated by the same standards used in rating the white schools.[21]

IMPROVEMENTS IN NEGRO SCHOOLS

It is noteworthy that the leaders of the PSTA during this very important period in the history of the Association not only constantly pressed for extension of educational opportunities to Negro pupils but also insisted upon being judged by the same criteria used in rating schools for white pupils. They were strenuously attempting to remove the "double standard" which was characteristic of the public school system in South Carolina. This persistence brought about some beneficial changes in the education of Negroes. Among them were the following:

1. Fortunately Superintendent Hope who was elected in 1923 gave more support to the improvement of Negro schools.

2. South Carolina was second only to North Carolina in the building of Rosenwald Schools. More money was voted for Negro school buildings in 1923 than in all the previous years. J. B. Felton, state agent for Negro schools, was the leader in this effort. His comments about the need for this action are as follows: "Ignorance and illiteracy cannot be banished from South Carolina by developing only one class of schools. To lift this state to a higher plane we must give all of the people a better opportunity to secure a common school education."[22]

3. A new school law known as the "6-0-1" law was enacted in 1925. This law guaranteed to every child in the state a seven-month school term.

4. A statewide teachers training program for Negro teachers was organized at State A and M College and the private colleges in the state.

5. The special Joint Committee of Negro teachers appointed by Mr. Swearengen in 1922 to standardize schools and colleges was continued by Dr. Hope. This Committee made annual reports to the state superintendents and to the PSTA.

These improvements in Negro schools support the observation made previously that the history of the PSTA reflects the progress or lack thereof which the state of South Carolina made in establishing a public school system for all the children of all the people. As more educational opportunities were extended, the stronger the organization became.

Other evidence of this strength may be found in the rapid growth of its membership and the constant changes which were made to meet emerging needs.

MEMBERSHIP GROWTH IN THE 1920's

The growth in membership was ample evidence of a remarkable awakening of Negro teachers. The number of members increased from 393 in 1920 to 1,724 in 1928. There were 3,360 Negro teachers in South Carolina in 1925. Of this number 1,244, or 37 percent, were enrolled. In 1926 the number increased to 1,560, or

43 percent of the total. By 1928 the membership increased to 1,724. Of special significance was the number of counties which enrolled 100 percent of their teachers in the Association.

In 1926 nine counties reported 100 percent enrollment—Richland, Anderson, Darlington, Marion, Dillon, Allendale, Fairfield, Georgetown, and Calhoun. The membership provision in the Constitution permitting 100 percent counties to keep 25 percent of the membership fee was serving its purpose. At this time there were only five counties with no members—Jasper, Lancaster, McCormick, Chesterfield, and Cherokee. In 1927 all of these counties except Cherokee sent in memberships. The Association gradually gained the support of all the counties. These figures were obtained from the reports of the executive secretary from 1920 to 1929.

NEED FOR ORGANIZATIONAL CHANGE

The Committee on Revision of the Constitution made the following changes which were adopted during the convention in March 1925:

1. The number of vice-presidents was increased from two to five and the provision which made county presidents vice-presidents of the state organization was deleted. The first group of officers to serve under this new arrangement were C. A. Lawson, president, and vice-presidents C. A. Johnson, J. L. Cain, A. A. Sims, Mrs. R. J. Clark, and Mrs. M. A. La Saine.

2. The Executive Committee was elected from the seven congressional districts rather than the total membership. This reduced the ten elective members of the committee to seven.

3. The Health and Physical Education Department was provided for in the by-laws.

In addition to these changes two new committees were created—a Committee on Systematizing Records and Reports and a Committee on Athletics. The Committee on Records and Reports detailed in 15 items how records should be kept and how funds should be received and disbursed.

In 1928 a number of changes occurred in policy and personnel. The cost of holding the 1927 convention in Greenville was so great that it was agreed that all future meetings of the Association be held in Columbia. Another policy change limited the president to two years and made him ineligible to succeed himself. The most significant personnel change was the resignation of President I. M. A. Myers, who had held the position since 1918. John P. Burgess was elected to serve in this capacity and held the position until 1940.

CONTINUED GROWTH IN THE 1930's

During the decade of the thirties the Palmetto State Teachers Association continued to grow in membership and in influence. In the March 1931 issue of the *Bulletin,* John P. Burgess, the executive secretary, reported an increase in membership in 1930 to 2,385. This represented an increase of 458 over the membership for 1929 when it had reached an all time high of 1,927.[23] Ten years later, by 1939–40, the enrollment increased to 5,488.[24] With one exception there was a steady increase each year. It is significant to note that the organization grew faster during the decade of the thirties than in the previous 30 years. The counties reporting 100 percent membership increased from nine in 1926 to thirty-eight in 1939–40. Only nine counties did not have every Negro teacher enrolled and four of those reported 75 percent membership. Over the six-year period from 1935 to 1941 the Palmetto State Teachers Association refunded $11,950.50 to 100 percent counties. This made the county organizations stronger; and as they increased in strength and influence, their leaders cooperated with the state officers and the Executive Committee in establishing a larger and more influential state organization.

The Palmetto State Teachers Association was also very fortunate in continuing to elect leaders of high calibre who were dedicated to the difficult task of building a profession which would improve the educational opportunities for black children and black teachers. Beginning with the Reverend A. A. Sims, principal of Sims High School in Union, South Carolina, the following persons guided the destiny of the organization in the capacity of president: Dr. C. A. Johnson, supervisor of Negro schools, Columbia; Dr. H. B. Butler, principal, Butler High School, Hartsville; Mr. C. V. Bing, principal, Allendale County Training School, Allendale; Mr. G. W. Howard, principal, Howard High School, Georgetown; and Dr. Gerard A. Anderson, principal, Wilson High School, Florence. All of these men served two-year terms as president of the Palmetto State Teachers Association from 1929 to 1940. Like their counterparts before them, they waged an unrelenting battle against the educational inequities in the state. One of the presidents stated his position this way:

> Our objectives are better salaries for Negro teachers, better schools and longer terms for Negro children, better facilities and better teachers for our children. We have gone as men to the legislature and there made contacts with members of that body, protesting against legislation discriminating to our group that was about to be adopted. The result was that the enacting words of a discriminatory nature were stricken out. We have appeared before the various officials and protested against the present salary setup. We have asked for longer terms and better schools and other conveniences.[25]

A special tribute should be paid to John P. Burgess, the executive secretary from 1928 to 1940, for his untiring efforts to build a strong association. He traveled extensively throughout the state and into every county soliciting membership and urging teachers and principals to support the efforts of the Association. He resigned from the position of executive secretary in 1940 when he was elected president of the Palmetto State Teachers Association.

The Reverend A. A. Sims, principal of Sims High School in Union and PSTA president, 1928-30.

Gerard A. Anderson, principal of Wilson High School in Florence and PSTA president, 1938-40.

GAINS IN PSTA PRESTIGE

In addition to the dedicated leadership which the Association had during the thirties, there were three other factors that contributed to the remarkable growth.

The number of qualified teachers increased. In 1925 there were only 3,360 Negro teachers, and most of them were poorly qualified. A survey of the statistics of the teachers examination given the following year revealed that 699 Negro applicants took the examination and only 64 earned certificates. However, none of the 64 earned first grade certificates. This was most discouraging to the leaders in education and to the parents of the children enrolled in public schools throughout the state. This was also a great challenge to the Negro teacher training institutions in the state. South Carolina State College, Claflin College, Morris College, Benedict College, Allen University, and other teacher training institutions cooperated in training better qualified teachers for the Negro schools in the state. By 1937 there were 5,007 Negro teachers in the state with 3,872, or 75 percent, holding first grade certificates. More than 22 percent had second grade certificates and only 17 held certificates of third grade.[26] This was remarkable progress in 10 years.

The awareness grew among Negro teachers that the Palmetto State Teachers Association was having some success in improving unfavorable educational conditions and that it was their best if not only hope for continued improvement in the future. For many years teachers did not feel that the Association championed their cause, and they were lukewarm in their support. When they got the message through their county associations that circumstances were improving and refunds were flowing back to counties for their own professional improvement, there was a new awakening among teachers throughout the state. The Palmetto State Teachers Association also gave financial support to the nine district summer schools which were upgrading teacher certification. This also raised the prestige of the Association among the state's Negro teachers.

Support from the Negro colleges increased. In the beginning only one institution of higher learning—South Carolina State College—gave more than token support to the Association. This was largely due to the fact that the second and fourth presidents of the Association were also presidents of South Carolina State College. After serving six years as president (longer than anyone except Mr. J. L.

Cain), Dr. Robert Shaw Wilkinson rendered very valuable service to the Association as chairman of the Executive Committee.

The *Teachers Directory of 1927–28* shows that only South Carolina State College and Allen University teachers held memberships in the Association. In 1937–38 the list included a substantial number of memberships from Allen University and Benedict, Claflin, State, and Friendship Colleges as well as Brainerd, Harbison, and Voorhees Institutes.[27] By 1940 Morris College also joined the list of two-and four-year colleges supporting the organization.

HOUSE OF DELEGATES: NEW GOVERNING BODY OF PSTA

Whenever an organization grows rapidly, changes become mandatory. The Palmetto State Teachers Association was no exception to this process. To give more of the growing number of members a voice in the governance of the organization, it became necessary to remove the major decision-making powers from the small group of 11 which constituted the Executive Committee and place the governance in a delegate assembly which represented all of the Association's constituents, namely the 46 counties and the institutions of higher learning. To realize this goal it became necessary to revise the constitution. In March 1935, the first revised and amended version was read to the Annual Convention. The principal difference was the creation of a House of Delegates that would be the governing body of the organization. However, it was not until March 1939 that the completely revised version was finally adopted by the convention. The members of the Constitution Committee were J. L. Cain, Dean K. W. Green, I. M. A. Myers, Dean N. C. Nix, and T. H. Pinckney. The most important provision of this constitution is Article V, which follows:

> Section 1. The House of Delegates shall consist of one delegate from each county where fifteen or more teachers have paid up for current year.
>
> Section 2. Each county having seventy-five to one hundred teachers, when sixty of these teachers are paid up in any current year, such a county is entitled to two delegates.

Section 3. Counties having two hundred or more paid up teachers for any current year are entitled to three delegates.

Section 4. No county shall have more than three delegates from the Public School System in the House of Delegates.

Section 5. Private schools or colleges with twenty or more teachers, 100% of said teachers having paid up in any current year, such school or college is entitled to one member in the House of Delegates.[28]

COOPERATION WITH OTHER ORGANIZATIONS

Another change observed during the decade of the thirties was the active cooperation of the Palmetto State Teachers Association with other organized groups interested in the welfare of children and the advancement of education. The first such organizations contacted by the Association were the Parent-Teacher Associations. On March 28, 1930, during the presidency of the Reverend A. A. Sims, the Resolution Committee submitted the following resolution:

> Be it resolved that the Palmetto State Teachers' Association now in session invite, through its Executive Committee, local Parent-Teacher Associations throughout South Carolina to send delegates to its next session for the purpose of organizing a permanent South Carolina State Parent-Teacher Association and working out plans to meet in the future with the Palmetto State Teachers' Association in its annual session—at the same time and place for mutual benefits, but separately as an organization.[29]

This resolution was adopted by the convention and both associations met jointly afterwards until 1962. The State Parent-Teacher Association held its annual meeting on the day prior to the annual convention of the Palmetto State Teachers Association.

Other organizations with which the Palmetto State Teachers Association sought cooperation and collaboration were the American Teachers Association, the National Education Association, and the Association of Negro Life and History. The affiliations will be discussed in more detail in Chapter XII.

CHAPTER III

1940-1946:
Steady Growth
Interrupted

Injustice anywhere is a threat to justice everywhere.

Martin Luther King, Jr.

When John P. Burgess was elected president of the Palmetto State Teachers Association in 1940, the Executive Committee appointed C. V. Bing, who served as president of the Association from 1935 to 1937, to the position of executive secretary. Mr. Bing served in this capacity until 1946 when the Palmetto State Teachers Association employed its first full-time executive secretary.

During this period from 1940 to 1946 the Association experienced some unexpected problems, the most serious being the outbreak of World War II. The attention of the nation was focused upon national defense. The state superintendent of education, James H. Hope, called upon the public school principals and teachers "to assume their part of the responsibility for the preparation of our nation in national defense in this critical period."[1]

In response to this appeal, the leaders of the Palmetto State Teachers Association selected such convention themes as "The School and National Defense" in 1941 and "The Role of the School in a Nation at War" in 1943. In addition to urging every Negro teacher to assist the Association in making its contribution to national defense, the Executive Committee decided that the 1943 annual convention would not be held. The April 1943 *Bulletin* contained the following references to this spirit:

> In times like these when many of our number are making the supreme sacrifice on the foreign battlefields of World War II, we,

61

at home, wish to do our share to help whenever and wherever we can.

Our Palmetto State Teachers Association is foregoing its annual meeting this historic year during the national emergency at the many requests of O.P.A. to preserve our supply of fuel and tires. The housing conditions in the Capital City have also become very acute since our last meeting.

Our bulletin is not as elaborate as in previous years due to the shortage of paper. . . .[2]

With the Palmetto State Teachers Association focusing most of its attention upon national defense and numbers of teachers joining the armed forces, there was a decided decline in membership. Teacher enrollment in the Association dropped from an all time high of 5,620 in 1941 to 4,750 in 1945. The reports of the executive secretary for this five-period were as follows: In 1941 there were 5,620 teachers holding memberships in the Association. In 1942 the number fell to 5,341; in 1943, to 4,776. There was a slight increase in 1944 to 4,980; but in 1945, it fell again to 4,750.

EQUALIZATION OF TEACHER SALARIES: A MAJOR ISSUE

World War II was no doubt the main reason for this tremendous drop in membership, but the Palmetto State Teachers Association also had another problem during this period which contributed in no small way to the reduction of teacher enrollment. This problem grew out of the growing trend toward militancy which was developing among the "young turks" who were growing tired of promises for educational equality which were not being fullfilled. The issue which concerned most of the so-called militants was the equalization of salaries.

The first time this matter was brought to the attention of the House of Delegates was in April 1941 when the Resolutions Committee included in its eight-point report that (1) teachers with similar training and performing the same class of work be paid the same salary; (2) complete equalization be made in two years; and (3) equalization begin in the 1941–1942 school term.[3]

The minutes of this meeting showing that these resolutions were adopted also state the following:

Rev. E. A. Adams, President of the local N.A.A.C.P. Chapter and Rev. J. P. Reeder, pastor, Zion Baptist Church, were present and they both took a few minutes to express their feelings on the big question with which the association is concerned—the equalification of teacher's salaries. They also expressed their sincere hopes that the Negro teachers will not accept any compromise and nothing less than equalization of salaries because it is JUST and RIGHT.[4]

The second time the issue of equalization of teachers salaries was discussed in the House of Delegates was on April 9, 1943 when the executive secretary, C. V. Bing, was summarizing his annual report. He mentioned an item of $1,200 to be taken out for a defense fund. It had been previously voted by the Executive Committee that the Association appropriate 25 percent of all money collected for the current year for this purpose after deducting the refund to counties. It had been voted also by the Executive Committee that $1,200 be set aside in 1943 for the teachers' Defense Fund. However, some members of the House of Delegates had not been informed of these actions, and a lengthy discussion followed Mr. Bing's reference to it. Finally a motion was made by the Reverend H. B. Butler that "$1,200 be used with the words Defense Fund meaning fighting for

C. V. Bing, principal of Allendale County Training School; PSTA president, 1935-37; and PSTA executive secretary, 1940-46.

J. T. W. Mims, principal of Bell Street High School and president of the Palmetto State Teachers Association, 1942-44.

equalization of salaries for teachers and transportation facilities and other facilities for Negro children to start this year."[5]

With an almost unanimous vote it would appear that this motion would be favorably implemented. However, such was not the case. The House of Delegates met again at five o'clock the same day (April 9), and the first item on the agenda was equalization of salaries. Twelve very influential members stated that they were not in favor of a court fight. This precipitated another lengthy discussion between those favoring a court suit and those opposing. J. T. W. Mims, who was president of the Association at this time, attempted to placate both factions by reading the report which a committee composed of himself, Dr. M. F. Whittaker of South Carolina State College, and C. C. Woodson of Spartanburg made to the state Board of Education and the governor on the morning of April 9:

> We are desirous that you close the gap between salaries of Negro and white teachers with a 50 percent differential. We are desirous that you give us at least two busses for each high school and at least one bus for each consolidated grammar school.[6]

President Mims then said that if these requests were met, the group would not resort to court action. Otherwise, the possibilities of keeping the Association out of court were very slim.

PROPOSED APPROPRIATION TO NAACP FOR SALARY EQUALIZATION FIGHT

Since the reply to this request was evasive, J. L. Dixon, who with Charles McIver and others were in favor of court action, made a motion that the Defense Fund of $1,200 be given to the state chapter of the NAACP in order to help the organization carry the fight for Negro teachers. He further stated that this fact was not to be published in the papers. Then the opposition began stalling tactics. There were several unreadinesses followed by a motion from J. E. Blanton that the motion be tabled indefinitely. It was seconded, and the vote was 39 for the motion and 31 against it. The suit was tabled.[7]

C. W. Madden made a motion that the chairman of the House of Delegates appoint a free conference committee from both sides to work with the Executive Committee to seek solution to the problem.

The motion was seconded and carried. The following persons were appointed: W. H. Neal, W. A. White, and C. W. Madden representing the opposing group and J. L. Dixon, Charles McIver, and L. V. Vance representing those favoring court action.

Equalization of teachers salaries was mentioned again in the House of Delegates on April 6 and 7, 1944. The Reverend H. B. Butler moved that "we turn the $1,200 'earmarked money' over this session to the NAACP of South Carolina to aid in the fight for equalization of teachers' salaries in the state of South Carolina."[8] The motion was carried. On the following day J. M. Hinton, president of the state NAACP, "spoke at length on the subject 'Equalization of Salaries for Negro Teachers' and the lack of the need to fear to lose jobs because of asking for constitutional rights."[9]

On April 7, 1945, Mr. J. M. Hinton spoke again to the House of Delegates on the salary inequality issue and cited differentials in the salary scale that the NAACP was determined to wipe out. He asked that the Association appoint a committee of seven to work with the NAACP Defense Committee in planning all future court action.[10] The motion to appoint such a committee was carried.

The minutes of the April 6 and 7 meetings reveal that the following persons were elected by their districts to serve on this special committee:

District 1. N. R. Harper, Robertsville School, Pineland

District 2. Isaac Bracy, Stone Hill School, Sumter

District 3. L. L. Pendarvis, Brewer High School, Greenwood

District 4. C. A. Reubens, Bell Street School, Clinton

District 5. J. R. Harper, Browning Home, Camden

District 6. B. A. Gary, Mayo High School, Darlington

The Reverend H. B. Butler of Allen University was elected by the body to represent the colleges.

Mr. Bracy then moved that $500 be appropriated to the NAACP immediately. It was seconded. Several unreadinesses were heard. H. C. Brewer then made a substitute motion that the delegates present at this convention be empowered with the authority to go back to their counties and ask the support of their teachers in the movement. The motion was seconded and carried by a vote of 23 to 8.

Then the Reverend C. H. Brown of Benedict College moved that this body make a donation of $400 to the NAACP. The motion was seconded and carried with the understanding that the $400 would be presented at the first meeting of the joint committee.

Mr. Hinton reported that the $1,200 from the Palmetto State Teachers Association was still in the bank and that there was a total of $2,304 in the fund to fight the case. He cited differentials in the salary scale and stated that the NAACP was determined to end this inequality.

It may not be apparent to those who did not experience the educational inequities of this period how seriously this fight for salary equalization affected the Palmetto State Teachers Association. In the first place it divided the Association into two factions. There were those (some in influential leadership positions) who did not believe in the use of force to attain this objective. They also felt that the NAACP was controlling the Association and that the Palmetto State Teachers Association was not in charge of its own program.

On the other hand the smaller and more militant faction had grown impatient with the superintendent of education, the state Board of Education, and the legislature for dragging their feet on this issue. They felt that force (not violence) was the only recourse now open to them to reach this important goal. Their position was clear—let the NAACP take the matter to court.

REPRISALS SUFFERED BY NAACP SUPPORTERS

This problem was further compounded by the attempts of the white power structure to find out which Negro teachers held membership in the NAACP. This was more evident in the rural areas and small towns than in the large cities. The Clarendon County case is a classic example of what happened to a strong supporter of the NAACP. The Reverend J. A. De Laine, a minister of the AME Church then living and serving a congregation in Lake City, was shot at, burned out, and forced to leave the state. There were numerous instances where Negro teachers lost their jobs because of their affiliation with the organization.

In 1945 J. T. W. Mims, at that time principal of Bell Street High School in Laurens and also president of the Palmetto State Teachers

Association from 1942 to 1944, was forced out of the public school system in South Carolina and was kept out for 10 years because of the leadership and support he gave the suit for equalization of teachers' salaries and the transportation suit that was filed later. Mr. Mims was chairman of the Transportation Committee which also included C. S. McIver of Summerville and Roy Cunningham of Florence.

Another Association president, J. T. McCain who served from 1946 to 1948, lost his position because of his support of the NAACP. At the time the action was taken Mr. McCain was principal of Palmetto High School in Mullins.

The Palmetto State Teachers Association then had to deal with a third factor—fear of reprisals upon their members if they instituted a court fight for equalization of salaries.

This writer recalls very vividly that the first question he was asked when being interviewed for an important administrative position was "Are you a member of the NAACP?" Whether my affirmative answer influenced the negative action taken by the all-white committee may never be known. It was extremely significant that my possible membership in the NAACP was more important to the members of the interviewing committee than my educational qualifications for the position. This experience was followed by two similar incidents: I was asked the same question by a county superintendent, and a trustee of a school board gave me the impression that there was an insidious witch hunt being carried on in some areas of the state to ferret out the supporters of the NAACP to weaken both it and the Palmetto State Teachers Association. It is one of the ironies of fate that the organization that created so much fear among county and state officials in the 1940's was the least objectionable of the civil rights organizations in the 1960's.

ACCOMPLISHMENTS OF THE EARLY FORTIES

In spite of these almost insurmountable problems, the Palmetto State Teachers Association managed to stay alive and actually engage in a number of constructive activities.

In 1941 John P. Burgess who was president at that time recommend that "the Executive Committee be instructed to take out a charter for the Palmetto State Teachers Association."[11] The matter was referred to the House of Delegates on April 3, 1941 and accepted without opposition. By this action the Palmetto State Teachers Association was incorporated. This was an important step.

In 1943 J. T. W. Mims, president, appointed two additional committees. There was an urgent need for the Association to have accurate information to intelligently plan for the future. To meet this need a Research and Investigation Committee was appointed with Dr. E. H. Fitchett of Claflin College as chairman. Equally as important was a mechanism to influence legislation favorable to education. To meet this need Mr. Mims appointed a Legislative Committee with B. W. Gallman as chairman.[12]

On April 7, 1945 President B. W. Gallman appointed a committee to draw up a petition to be submitted to the governor, superintendent of education, all state supervisors and the speaker of the house. He suggested that the petition contain the following items:

1. Equal transportation facilities for all high school pupils.

2. Full enforcement of the Compulsory School Law.

3. The same or equal opportunity for higher education on the undergraduate and graduate levels.

4. Qualified Negro representation in the state Department of Education.

5. A request made to all members of the United States Senate and the House from South Carolina petitioning them to support federal aid to education.[13]

Most of these items on this petition were being officially mentioned for the first time and represent a broader scope than the burning issue of equalization of salaries. They laid the foundation for the constructive program which followed.

During this period Association officials gave serious attention to the recertification of teachers. Helping teachers prepare themselves for the anticipated examination was uppermost in their minds.[14]

The problems with which the Association was confronted during the forties along with the urgent need to implement the new policies created a special need for a full-time executive secretary for the Association. The desirability of employing such a person had been stated before. At this stage in the development of the organization the position was no longer just desirable, it was mandatory.

CHAPTER IV

1946-1950: Planned Professional Growth

By uniting we stand; by dividing we fall.

John Dickenson

Fortunately for the cause of education in South Carolina the Palmetto State Teachers Association survived the divisive factors it experienced in the early forties, from 1940 to 1945. During the last five years of the decade unity was restored, and the Association embarked upon a period of expansion and preparation for more extensive service unmatched in its history. The most important single reason for unification of the organization was the planned professional growth which placed the implementation of the Association's program above the special concerns of any single administration. The constitution limited the number of years a president could serve the Association to a two-year term, which was not long enough for one administration to make a significant impact on the organization. There was an urgent need for longer and more sustained emphasis on the attainment of the goals of the Association. This, of necessity, created a need for long-range planning on the part of the leadership both present and future.

PRESIDENT GALLMAN'S TEN-POINT PROGRAM

This planning began during the second year of the presidency of B. W. Gallman. In 1945 Mr. Gallman proposed a ten-point, five-year program for the Palmetto State Teachers Association which was adopted by the Executive Committee and approved by the House of Delegates. This action was tantamount to a commitment of future presidents to these specific goals for a minimum of five years. It eventually took longer to achieve all of them, but the important first step was taken and continuity of effort was assured.

The ten-point program was as follows:

1. Purchase a piece of property for headquarters for the Palmetto State Teachers Association.

2. Employ a full-time executive secretary.

3. Publish a professional journal to serve as the official voice of the organization.

4. Promote qualified Negro representation in the state Department of Education and all other groups and committees dealing with the educational affairs of the state.

5. Cooperate more closely with teachers' associations of other states.

6. Increase the membership of South Carolina teachers in the American Teachers Association.

7. Support equality of educational opportunity on all levels of education.

8. Extend the services of the Palmetto State Teachers Association to more of its members.

9. Support federal aid to education.

10. Increase annual dues from $1.00 to $1.50 and eliminate refunds to counties, private schools, and colleges.[1]

FULL-TIME EXECUTIVE SECRETARY

The implementation of this ten-point program began July 1, 1945 after Mr. Gallman began the second year of his presidency. Although a firm foundation for the future was laid during his administration, only two of the goals were realized before his term ended in 1946. One was the employment of a full-time executive secretary. When this matter was being discussed in the House of Delegates on April

5, 1946, S. L. Finley asked Mr. Gallman to give a full interpretation of the meaning of a full-time secretary. Mr. Gallman's answer was as follows:

> A full-time Secretary means a man or woman, who will spend or devote full time as a secretary; in other words, a person who has no outside interests that will take his time from the work of the Association.[2]

Following this interpretation, Eli J. Davis, speaking for the Executive Committee, presented the name of Alfred T. Butler, Sr., as executive secretary. After a brief discussion he was approved by the House of Delegates by a vote of 35 to 17. It was later requested that the House of Delegates give its unanimous vote to the newly elected executive secretary. A motion was made, seconded, and carried to this effect, and Butler became the first full-time executive secretary of the Palmetto State Teachers Association.[3] This was such a significant event that it ushered in a new era in the history of the organization. A need that had been discussed unofficially for 16 years had finally become a reality.

INCREASE IN DUES

The other goal realized during Mr. Gallman's presidency was an increase in the membership dues to pay the expenses of the new office. His recommendation was to increase the dues from $1.00 to $1.50 per member; however, that would not provide enough funds to underwrite the costs of the office. The final decision made by the House of Delegates in March 1945 was to increase the dues to $2 per member and discontinue all refunds to counties, private schools, and colleges.[4]

During the presidency of J. T. McCain three additional goals of this ten-point program were attained: equalization of teacher salaries (see Chapter XIII for specific events leading to the attainment of this goal), purchase of a headquarters building, and publication of a different kind of journal.

SALARY EQUALIZATION

The new proposed state aid salary schedule enacted into law by the South Carolina General Assembly was presented to the House of

Delegates on November 30, 1946. It was unanimously adopted by the delegates. The Council of Delegates of the South Carolina Education Association also unanimously adopted the measure.[5] This new salary schedule was a high-water mark in the history of education in South Carolina in that it marked the first time that the state made any attempt to equitably distribute salaries based on training and experience. While it was a giant step in the right direction, there were some critics of the legislation who felt that the schedule was somewhat discriminatory when they discovered that a teacher examination was required to determine the grade of certificate the teacher would receive. It was pointed out that Negro teachers were still handicapped by the separate but unequal education they had received from the state, and many would not be able to qualify for the higher paying certificates. Additionally, it was stated that white teachers had more opportunities to take graduate work in South Carolina and that with the exception of limited opportunities for graduate study at South Carolina State College, Negro teachers had to leave the state to get the graduate training required for the Class 1 and 2 Certificates for which higher salaries were paid. In spite of these criticisms the new salary schedule was regarded as a significant improvement over the previous certification procedures used by the state Department of Education.

J. T. McCain, dean of Morris College in Sumter and PSTA president, 1946-48.

B. W. Gallman, Palmetto State Teachers Association president, 1944-46.

This two-story frame building was purchased in 1947 by the Association to serve as its first permanent headquarters. Located at 1719 Taylor Street in Columbia, it housed the administrative offices of the Association, a conference room for committee meetings, and rooms rented out to provide income. This structure was torn down to make way for the new headquarters building constructed in 1957.

PSTA HEADQUARTERS BUILDING

The purchase of a headquarters building at 1719 Taylor Street by the Palmetto State Teachers Association was another phase of the ten-point program realized during the administration of Mr. McCain. It was an ideal location in that it was just three doors from the Township Auditorium where the general meetings of the conventions were held and within a walking distance of five blocks from Benedict College and Allen University where most departmental meetings were arranged. The first floor was large enough to provide an office for the executive secretary, an office for the secretary to the executive secretary, a meeting room for the Executive Committee, a utility room, and a powder room for ladies.

The second floor provided office space for the Jeanes teacher for Richland County, the Richland County Tuberculosis Association, the Southern Automobile Association, a music-book store, and a lounge for men.[6]

The purchase of this building finally gave the Association a "home" in Columbia and stimulated a greater and stronger loyalty to the Association from its membership.

PSTA EDUCATION NEWS REPLACES BULLETIN

Another goal of the ten-point program which was partially realized during McCain's administration was the publication of a professional journal. In October 1946 the first issue of the *Palmetto State Teachers Association Education News* was published, replacing the *Bulletin*. It was not the scholarly professional journal to which the Association was aspiring, but it did have these desirable features: (1) it was published quarterly rather than once a year; (2) research studies and other articles of interest to education were published; and (3) it served as the official voice of the Association.

The format was that of a tabloid newspaper, and it achieved a wider circulation than the *Bulletin*. A part of the cost of publication came from the increased dues rather than entirely from advertisement income. The executive secretary served as the editor and the Executive Committee was listed as the publisher. The publication maintained this form until 1951.

PRESIDENT McCAIN IN 1946:
FIVE NEW GOALS

Immediately upon his election to the presidency, J. T. McCain had an "Open Letter" to the Palmetto State Teachers Association members published in the October 1946 issue of the *Education News*. In this letter he makes the following statement:

> I am very anxious that the Palmetto State Teachers Association rank with the better Teachers Associations of America and to do this, I am asking the cooperation of all of our teachers, so that our association can be felt throughout the U.S.[7]

Mr. McCain requested the assistance of every teacher in South Carolina to urge the House of Delegates to act upon the following problems in addition to the ten-point program the Association adopted in 1945: consolidation of small rural schools where possible, transportation for all South Carolina children where needed, tenure for teachers, higher retirement funds for all teachers, nine-month school term for all teachers, and the accrediting of all Negro high schools.[8]

These problems were discussed by the delegates on November 30, 1946, and five items were selected for special action:

1. Consolidation

2. Transportation

3. Compulsory school attendance

4. Representation of qualified Negroes in the state Department of Education and on the state Board of Education

5. Larger appropriations for the graduate school of South Carolina State A and M College in Orangeburg.[9]

A committee was appointed to assist in the implementation of these five goals. All except qualified Negro representation at the state level were new areas of endeavor for the Association. B. W. Gallman, chairman of the Legislative Committee and former PTSA president, was asked to serve as chairman of the committee. The other members were A. Maceo Anderson, I. C. Bracy, Mrs. M. B. Thomas, J. R. Harper, W. M. Bankhead, and A. T. Butler.[10]

1948–1950: PRESIDENT POTTS
EXPANDS GOALS

John F. Potts, former vice-president and chairman of the Program Committee, succeeded J. T. McCain as president of the Palmetto State Teachers Association in 1948. Having worked closely with Mr. Gallman and Mr. McCain, he was strongly committed to the ten-point program inaugurated during Gallman's administration and the five goals established during the presidency of Mr. McCain. Some of the more significant accomplishments during his administration were as follows:

1. The fulfillment of his election promise to pay in full the balance due on the headquarters building. The total cost of the building and land was $10,000. Renovations and furnishings cost an additional $2,651.07. The down payment on the house was $4,000 and the unpaid balance as of July 1, 1948 was $6,000. This was paid in full in April 1949.[11]

2. A closer cooperation with other teacher associations was effected when the Palmetto State Teachers Association joined the Conference of State Teachers and Education Association Officials which was organized in February 16, 1947. This

John F. Potts, principal of Avery Institute in Charleston and PSTA president, 1948-50.

organization represented many thousands of teachers in the 17 states having separate schools for Negro children and took a firm stand in presenting the cause of the teachers in Negro schools before the United States Congress, the various state legislatures, and wherever the voice of the Negro teacher needed to be heard.[12]

3. Memberships of teachers in the Palmetto State Teachers Association were significantly increased in the American Teachers Association. When the forty-fifth annual convention was held in Atlantic City in 1949, the Palmetto State Teachers Association ranked third from the top of the list of states holding memberships. In addition, three PSTA members served as officers. John F. Potts, principal of Avery Institute, served as vice-president and regional director and Frank A. De Costa, dean of the graduate school of South Carolina State College, and Guerney E. Nelson, dean of Benedict College, served as state directors of South Carolina. The incessant work of these officers and executive secretary Butler resulted in the Palmetto State Teachers Association becoming one of the leading parent bodies in the American Teachers Association. Only Alabama and Maryland ranked above South Carolina in influence and memberships.[13]

4. Special assistance was given to the enactment of the Taft–McCowen Bill which provided federal aid to education. As the drive for enactment reached its final stage in January 1948, the Legislative Committee used every means at its command to urge congressmen to cast a favorable vote for the legislation.

There were still three goals of the original ten-point program which were not fully realized. Two were partially attained—equality of educational opportunities, and increased service to members. Some progress was made in both areas, but they were too comprehensive to become realities in a five-year period. The appointment of qualified Negroes to positions in the state Department of Education was the last goal to see progress.

In November 1948, President Potts made a report to the House of Delegates concerning this matter:

... a committee composed of Mr. Gallman, the Executive Secretary and himself had held a conference by appointment with the State Superintendent concerning bus transportation and representation in the State Department of Education. The committee had tried to make it plain that they wanted something done before the suit came up regarding bus transportation. Replies were non-committal and evasive. It was implied that something would be done concerning transportation and that there were interviews with from one to three persons for State Department appointments. President Potts emphasized that everything said was very evasive.[14]

Mr. Gallman stated that although the Palmetto State Teachers Association had made several efforts to attain this goal, the results had been disappointing.[15]

Finally in the fall of 1949, W. T. Gantt of the Ridge Hill School was appointed to the state Department of Special Education to work with Mr. Agnew in sight and hearing therapy.[16] This was not the appointment the Association had anticipated but the persistence of the administrations from Gallman to Potts in implementing the ten-point program of the Association finally got results. Some progress was made in each of the ten areas.

In the president's annual address to the Association in 1949, Mr. Potts stated:

The significant thing about the program of the Association is that it does not change with each administration because each builds on the ground work laid by his predecessor until the objectives are attained. This gives our program the continuity it must have if we are going to meet the educational needs of pupils, teachers and adults in the Palmetto State.[17]

Like his predecessors, Mr. Potts also suggested additional goals for consideration for the future. Some of these were previously stated, partially attained goals; and others were new. Some of the new goals were as follows:

1. A minimum salary of $2,400 throughout the state.

2. A more adequate retirement plan.

3. A teacher-recruiting program.

4. More effective tenure legislation to provide professional security.[18]

During this administration strong emphasis was placed upon the professional development of teachers at all levels—the Annual Convention, the district and county meetings—with de-emphasis on the political activities.[19]

Organization of the first state chapter of the Future Teachers of America was at the Annual Convention on March 25, 1949. Representatives from Allen University and Benedict, Claflin, Morris, and South Carolina State Colleges were in attendance at this meeting and elected Miss Trudelle Wimbush as the sponsor.[20] The first high school FTA chapters also were organized that year.

In 1948–49 the Association for the first time operated on a prepared budget and employed a certified public accountant to audit the books. These actions assured the members that the financial affairs of the Association were being handled in a business-like way.[21]

PSTA GROWTH IN NUMBERS AND STRENGTH

The last five years of the decade from 1940 to 1950 may be described as a period of "educational renaissance." The Association not only recovered from the decline it experienced between 1940 and 1945, but emerged stronger, more united, and more influential than ever before in its history. The only dark cloud on the horizon was the unfavorable publicity the Association received during the investigation of cheating on the teacher examination. The Executive Committee held two meetings to discuss the matter and issued a statement condemning the unethical practice of those who cheated on the examination and offered assistance to those wrongfully accused.[22]

Even this unfortunate occurrence did not hinder the growth of the Association. After the membership dropped to 4,750 in 1945, having reached an all time high of 5,620 in 1941, there was a steady rise in memberships. By 1947 the memberships had increased to 5,227. In 1948 the number grew to 5,613. By 1949 the enrollment reached the highest number in the history of the Association—5,848.

In addition, the Association gained strength in other ways:

1. The constitution was revised to provide two meetings a year of the House of Delegates. One was held when the Annual Convention was in session and the other was held in the

fall, usually in November. This was a very desirable change in that decisions could be made more rapidly and the business of the Association could be conducted in a more efficient way.

2. More emphasis was placed upon research. During this four-year period from 1946 to 1950, research papers prepared by Dr. W. R. Harrison and Dr. J. E. Briggs of Benedict College, Dr. Frank De Costa, Dr. Herman W. Sartor of South Carolina State College, and others appeared in the *Education News.*

3. A Placement Bureau was established to aid teachers in getting positions.

4. Memberships from Palmetto State Teachers Association in the National Education Association increased significantly. Negroes were included in the South Carolina delegation to the NEA convention for the first time in 1948.

   Still another evidence of professional growth was the affiliation of the Greenville City Teachers Association with the National Education Association. According to Mrs. Alberta Grimes, who was one of the organizers and the first president of the organization, "this was the first all Black local association in South Carolina to have this National Education Association affiliation and one hundred percent membership in the Palmetto State Teachers Association." This affiliation entitled the local association to be represented at the annual national conventions. Delegates were sent beginning in 1949.

5. Two new committees were appointed, a Legislative Committee and a Committee on Research and Investigation.

6. There was a closer collaboration between the Palmetto State Teachers Association and the NAACP. A committee from the House of Delegates continued to work with a committee of the NAACP to eliminate educational inequities through legal action. The Defense Fund increased to $3,500 in 1948.

7. The House of Delegates increased the membership dues from $2 to $3 per member in 1948.

8. An official emblem of the Palmetto State Teachers Association was designed by Guerney E. Nelson, Jr., a student at Carver High School in Columbia. The emblem included a palmetto tree representing the state; an open book, the principal tool of teachers; a lighted candle, signifying the light of knowledge; and the Latin words *sit lux* which mean "let there be light." The House of Delegates voted unanimously to adopt the design as the official emblem of the Association.[23]

9. A yearbook was published by the Department of Elementary School Principals of the Palmetto State Teachers Association.

10. Professional standards were elevated, and professional growth was stimulated.

The emphasis on professional growth was perhaps the most significant of all of the contributions of this period. In some of the previous years the group meetings were very poorly attended because politics had a greater appeal than professional growth. When the Association decided to spend more of its funds for consultative services and bring to South Carolina well-known resource persons and consultants on all levels for all departments, the rooms were too small to hold the teachers who attended. As one president put it, "Our Association is more of an institute than Easter Parade."[24]

This concentration on professional growth also had a very favorable effect upon the House of Delegates. Because many of them wanted to attend the professional meetings, the long wrangles, disputes, and heated discussions were discontinued and the business of the Association was transacted in a dignified and intelligent manner. The House was able to take care of the business of the Association and still attend the professional meetings.

Another important feature of this professional growth was the observance of the convention theme in the district and county meetings. Much of what was learned at the Annual Convention filtered down to the districts and counties and from there to the classroom.

The Program Committee made its report in November when the House of Delegates met and it was discussed on the county and district level until the next November. This planned professional growth was augmented by reports from the Code of Ethics Committee. In this way the Association elevated standards as it stimulated professional growth.[25]

CHAPTER V

1950-1960: Expanding and Organizing for Action

Sail On, O Ship of State!
Sail On, O Union, strong and great!
Humanity with all its fears,
With all the hopes of future years,
Is hanging breathless on thy fate.

Henry Wadsworth Longfellow

Probably the most significant contribution to the growth and development of the Palmetto State Teachers Association between 1946 and 1950 was the employment of a full-time executive secretary. All of the officers and members of the Executive Committee, the House of Delegates, and standing committees had full-time positions and could not assume the daily responsibilities for the efficient operation of the Association. No matter how excellent the intentions of the leaders were or how well they planned for the future, a full-time secretary was needed to implement the decisions resulting from planning and execute the recommendations made and approved by the presidents, committees, and governing bodies of the organization.

A. T. BUTLER, FIRST FULL-TIME EXECUTIVE SECRETARY

As indicated in the preceding chapter, the first full-time executive secretary was A. T. Butler, Sr. He was a very capable and aggressive

83

administrator who worked closely with the presidents, the Executive Committee, and the House of Delegates in helping the Association reach its goals. As the official voice of the Association he spoke out against the inequities in education in South Carolina.[1]

He was instrumental in building the membership to 5,900 in 1949—an all-time high for the Association. He was also very active in other professional organizations, especially the National Education Association and the American Teachers Association.

1950: EXECUTIVE SECRETARY SOLOMON BEGINS SERVICE

When Mr. Butler resigned in June 1950, the Association operated without the services of an executive secretary for a period of six months. Walker E. Solomon, who succeeded him, was not selected until November 11, 1950 and did not begin his duties until December 1950. Further evidence of the importance of this position may be found in the brief decline in the growth of the organization during this six-month period. The membership dropped from an all-time high of 5,900 in March 1949 to 5,100 in March 1950. Also adversely affecting the Association at this time was the teacher examination cheating episode which received wide publicity and spawned numerous rumors.

History has proven that the selection of Mr. Solomon was a wise decision. He assumed his duties during unsettled times and worked diligently to check the temporary decline and move the organization forward again. During his tenure of office the Palmetto State Teachers Association eventually experienced unprecedented progress and unparalleled growth. By 1952–53, the membership had increased to 5,800 and rose steadily after that. Probably the most significant contribution made during this period was the expansion of the Association's services to many more of its constituents. Mr. Solomon cannot be given enough credit for his untiring efforts and administrative skill in planning on-going programs and services for adult and youth members.

1950–1952: PRESIDENT PARLER'S PROGRAM

The first president to make use of Mr. Solomon's services was J. C. Parler, principal of Wilkinson High School in Orangeburg, who assumed office on July 1, 1950. Mr. Parler had been struggling valiantly to keep the Association moving forward without the services of an executive secretary. In one of his messages to the teachers he made the following appeal:

> Never has a single hour in the history of the Palmetto State Teachers Association been more important to the future of the organization than this hour. . . . As you look upon the uncertainties of the present and with both eyes cast upon the future, may your heart say to you, "Now is the time to strive more valiantly than ever not only to keep alive, but also to make more effective and far reaching the work of the only organization in the state which represents all of our school administrators, teachers, children and patrons in a common cause."[2]

Mr. Parler was delighted to have Mr. Solomon's assistance in rebuilding the Palmetto State Teachers Association. On January 6, 1951 the president and the executive secretary called a meeting of all the county presidents to have them hear Mr. Parler's recommended "Program for the Palmetto State Teachers Association for 1951–52." Of the 46 county presidents, 37 were present. In giving the purpose of the meeting, Mr. Solomon told the presidents, "You

J. C. Parler, principal of Wilkinson High School in Orangeburg and PSTA president, 1950-52.

are the source of information for your Association, and the effectiveness of the State Association's program will depend upon the impartial interpretation you give each item in discussing it with your teachers in monthly meetings."[3]

This meeting brought about two far-reaching results— the county presidents voiced complete approval of the Program and voted to create a permanent organization to assist in implementing the Program in each county. The following officers were elected:

President—H. H. Marshall, principal, Saluda Rosenweld High School

Vice-president—Clinton I. Young, principal, Buist Elementary School

Secretary—Leila A. Bradby, Schofield High School

Treasurer—J. R. Ezell

The Program for 1951–52 recommended by Mr. Parler is submitted in its entirety. It is somewhat reptitious in that it contains a number of recommendations submitted by previous presidents. The reason for including the full statement is that Mr. Parler provides a good rational for each item of the program. It is also broader in scope than most of the previous programs.

Program of the Palmetto State Teachers Association, 1951–1952

I. Increase in salaries of all school personnel: administrators, teachers, etc.

A. The State of South Carolina must make provisions to pay teachers and administrators more money. The high cost of living makes this imperative.
B. There are various sources of possible revenue, however we believe that the 3 percent sales tax is the fairest way of raising money for paying teachers and administrators salaries that are commensurate with the high cost of living.

II. Qualified representation in the State Department of Education, on the State Board of Education, and all committees dealing with statewide educational affairs.

A. It is expedient that classroom teachers and lay people, as well as administrators, be given opportunity to serve all children of the State.
B. Opportunity for appointment to various positions such as State Agent of Schools, Elementary School Supervisor, Secondary School Supervisor, etc. should be extended to all administrators, classroom teachers, and lay people.

III.   A teacher recruiting program.

A.   Conferences should be conducted to attract persons of adequate scholastic ability, good character, and outstanding personality to the teaching profession.

B.   Public and private scholarship funds should be made available for assistance in the education of worthy prospective teachers who need financial help.

IV.   Professional security for teachers and administrators guaranteed by effective tenure legislation.

A.   An adequate tenure law should be passed to protect the teacher.

B.   Legal safeguards should be set up to define the relationship of the teacher to the school system or the state.

C.   Professional security guaranteed by effective legislation will enable efficient teachers to remain on the job of their choice. It will also provide the dismissed teacher with adequate knowledge of the reasons for the action of the Board of Trustees in her particular case. Eventually the rapid teacher turnover in South Carolina should be reduced.

V.   Equal educational opportunity for every child in South Carolina.

VI.   Permits to teach in South Carolina should be discontinued by July 1, 1951.

A.   For the last five years there has been a teacher education and certification program operative in South Carolina. Under the program provision is made to staff the schools with the highest quality of teachers possible.

B.   Since there is no teacher shortage, among our group in the state, the permit (which invites unqualified teachers to assume and maintain positions in our schools) should be eliminated.

VII.   Each teacher in the state should secure his registration certificate by the first Monday in February.

A.   Every teacher in South Carolina who fails to cast an intelligent vote in local, state, and national elections should be ashamed to remain a teacher. Teachers are under moral obligation to practice good citizenship in order to effectively teach, through living examples, the code of good citizenship.

B.   Through precept and example we shall not only encourage the boys and girls entrusted to our care to become good citizens, but we shall also, through them, reach into their homes and emphasize the importance of exercising citizenship rights by registering and voting.

VIII.   Sabbatical and sick leave should be made available for teachers.

A.   Sabbatical leave with pay will provide teachers with periods of rest, study, travel, and time for other professional improvement.

B.   Leave for personal sickness with full pay will provide teachers when they are physically unfit for classroom work.

IX.   Recommendations

A.   *Publications:* Beginning with the next issue of the "Palmetto State Teachers News," I recommend, at the same intervals, a journal with the approximate size 9 X 12 carrying the same type of news, also research and project work. The journal will be devoted to the economic, vocational, or financial welfare of the teachers of South Carolina. The journal could very well be called *The Journal of the Palmetto State Teachers Association.*

B. *Administrators:* (1) I recommend that a plan of action be worked out at once to create a department of elementary principals. (2) That the South Carolina administrators group be affiliated with the Palmetto State Teachers Association, (secondary principals and college administrators) maintaining its same construction, etc.

C. *Classroom teachers:* I recommend that a department of classroom teachers be organized at once. This gives the teachers of our association a greater voice in helping to plan and formulate procedures, etc.

D. *County presidents:* (1) If our programs are to be effective, our county presidents must be organized immediately into an association of county presidents. Through the president's association, the program can be carried directly to the teachers on a local as well as a state level. (2) The county president will have an opportunity of meeting with the teachers of his county each month and will be informed as to the contents of the program.

E. *Committees:* I recommend a committee to be appointed by the president to survey the needs and desires of the teachers of the state concerning policies and programs of the Palmetto State Teachers Association.

F. *Headquarters:* I recommend that a plan of action get underway now to renovate Headquarters, or that the present building be replaced by a new structure. As you know the building is in shape now where the Association will have to spend money in order to hold it together, and it still does not add to the looks or increase its value. In going over the building with an architect to try to estimate what is needed to fix it right and make it attractive as well, it would take at least $5,000. To brick up the outside it will take an additional $3,500. The income for the fiscal year will not allow such an expenditure.

G. *Increasing membership dues:* (1) I recommend that beginning with the school session 1951–52 the membership fee be increased from $3.00 to $7.00. If this is done the Association could sponsor a legislative information program to keep teachers alert relative to all matters taken up in the legislature pertaining to the teachers and the schools of South Carolina. A paid attorney could be maintained to carry on the work and to advise the Executive Committee and House of Delegates as to recommendations to be made to the legislature and issues on which the Association could take a stand. (2) An increase in dues would permit an increase in appropriation for active research and investigation. A progress report of research and investigation could be made in each issue of the journal. (3) An increase in dues would also permit an allocation of sufficient funds for expanding group activities during the annual convention.[4]

It is interesting to note the special emphasis Mr. Parler placed on registration and voting. The writer recalls that during the forties and the fifties the leaders of the Association urged each member to do three things. The first admonition was to obtain a membership card in the Palmetto State Teachers Association, the second was a membership in the National Association for the Advancement of Colored People, and the third was a registration certificate to vote. After complying with these three requests, the member was asked to join the National Education Association and the American Teachers Association.

There were a number of other significant achievements which occurred during Mr. Parler's presidency. Among them were the following:

1. The name of the official publication was changed from the *Education News* to the *Journal of the Palmetto State Teachers Association*. It was to be published bi-monthly rather than quarterly, and the format was changed to give the publication the appearance of a journal rather than a newspaper. The first issue was published in January 1951. In addition to the Association's news, the *Journal* published feature stories and articles of interest to teachers.

2. The Association adopted a Code of Ethics. This was designed to help the Association regain the prestige which was somewhat impaired by the unethical practices connected with the teacher examination in 1949.

3. The South Carolina High School and College Bandmasters Association was organized in 1950 at the State Agricultural and Industrial College. Reginald Thomasson, bandmaster of State Agricultural and Industrial College, was elected the first president of the organization which became a special department of the Palmetto State Teachers Association.

4. The membership fee was increased from $3 to $5 to more adequately finance the expanding organization. Mr. Parler recommended that the fee be increased to $7 a year. However, when his Program for 1951–52 was presented to the House of Delegates for their approval, this recommendation was changed from $7 to $5. This was the only change in the proposed program. All other items of the program including the specific recommendation were approved by the body.

5. A Building Committee was appointed by Mr. Parler to plan the erection of a new headquarters building. To finance this project the Policy Committee recommended to the House of Delegates in the spring of 1952 that 20 percent of the membership receipts ($1 out of every $5) be reserved to pay for the construction of the new facility. The recommendation was adopted.

6. Another significant milestone was reached by the Association in 1952 when Mrs. Sylvia Swinton was appointed supervisor of Negro Elementary Schools by the state Department of Education. The Palmetto State Teachers Association strenuously urged that this action be taken as far back as 1945. This was one item of Mr. Gallman's original "ten-point program." Token acknowledgement of this request was made in 1949 when W. T. Gantt was appointed to the state Department of Special Education to work with Mr. Agnew in sight and hearing therapy. However, the Association expected appointments of qualified Negroes in much more responsible positions. It took seven years of constant urging to realize all of the original ten-point program items adopted by the Association in 1945.

W. E. Solomon, executive secretary of the Association from 1950 through the 1967 merger, with the Building Committee, 1953. *Left to right:* M. D. Bogan, N. R. Harper, E. Russell, Mr. Solomon, J. A. Dorman, H. H. Marshall, and J. R. Harper.

1952-1954: PRESIDENT BOWEN AND PERIOD OF CHANGES

When John R. Bowen was elected president of the Palmetto State Teachers Association in 1952, he expressed a strong desire to implement the projects and recommendations which Mr. Parler had already proposed and the House of Delegates had adopted. Just as J. T. McCain and John F. Potts devoted the major portion of their two-year terms to the achievement of the goals the Association adopted during the presidency of B. W. Gallman, Mr. Bowen visualized his role as an implementor of a program already in progress rather than a proposer of a new program. In his first report to the House of Delegates he made this point very clear. He stated that "he would make every effort to adhere to an unwritten policy of Palmetto Education Association presidents, continuity of program from one administration to the next." He emphasized that he was particularly concerned with stabilizing the increased organizational activity of the Association.[5]

EDUCATIONAL CHANGES IN THE STATE

To get a deeper appreciation of the accomplishments of the leaders of the Association during this period from 1952 to 1954, a brief look at the total educational scene in South Carolina should be taken. Actually the state was undergoing an educational revolution. Since the court decrees of May 1951, the state of South Carolina was making rapid changes in an effort to equalize educational facilities and opportunities for black students. The governor and the superintendent of education were pressing the legislature to act promptly upon equality *before* the United State Supreme Court decided the constitutionality of racial segregation. Governor Brynes stated that if the Supreme Court failed to uphold segregation, the state would "reluctantly" abandon its public school system. The 1890 Supreme Court decision stated that segregation was permissible if equal facilities were provided for both races. However, the responsible education officials in South Carolina neglected this duty for more than 60 years. They waited too late to attempt to reach equality. Beginning in 1951 the following changes occurred in rapid succession:

1. The Governor recommended and the legislature adopted a 3 percent sales tax for a program of construction, improved transportation facilities, and increased teachers' salaries. In his inaugural address, Governor James R. Brynes stated "preference in construction should be given where the need is greatest. Fifty percent of the building program should be for schools for colored children."[6]

2. The Educational Finance Commission working with the school boards reduced the 1,220 school districts in South Carolina to 101. Each of the 46 counties had to reorganize before they could share in the $75,000,000 educational improvement program. Unfortunately 42 percent of the citizens of the state because they were Negroes had no voice in the expenditures. Neither were they represented on the 46 county boards of education responsible for the school district reorganization.

In less than three years after the sales tax was passed by the legislature, the Supreme Court on May 17, 1954 decreed that segregated schools are unconstitutional and that the doctrine of separate but equal is no longer valid.

This was the educational milieu in which the Palmetto State Teachers Association operated in the early fifties. These unprecedented changes had a tremendous impact upon the Association and the education of Negroes throughout the state. Even though equality of facilities and expenditures was not even remotely reached, some of the results of these efforts were favorable. Among them were the following:

1. The physical facilities for Negro children were tremendously improved.

2. Consolidation eliminated some of the weaker schools and strengthened those which were retained.

3. Bus transportation was made a statewide system and extended to much larger numbers of Negro students.

4. Teachers salaries were increased.

5. The elimination of 1,119 districts through consolidation increased the operational efficiency and raised the quality of instruction.

All of these improvements further support the theme that is continuously referred to in this history—the Palmetto State Teachers Association reflects the progress the state made in extending and improving the educational opportunities and facilities of all of the children of all of the people. There is a direct correlation between the progress of the Association and action of the legislature, the state Board of Education, and the state and county superintendents.

PSTA GROWTH WITH CHANGE

While these educational changes were occurring throughout the state, the Association under the leadership of President Bowen was also experiencing some far-reaching changes. Among the most significant were the following:

1. The departments became permanently organized and subject area groups were increased from 12 to 24. Arrangements were also made to have all department heads meet in October of each year to plan for the professional growth of their members. (For further elaboration see Chapter XI.)

2. The Palmetto State Teachers Association standing committees increased from 8 to 15.

3. Beginning in 1952, four newsletters were sent to the membership in addition to the five issues of the *Journal* which began in January 1951.

4. The areas of service were divided into seven fields. In September of 1952 Mr. Solomon, at the request of President Bowen to strengthen the organizational structure of the Association, prepared a special bulletin entitled *P.S.T.A.'s Services.*

The various services the Association rendered its members were listed in this special service bulletin according to the following seven categories:

Field Work: This area was concerned with increasing memberships, advising local units about salary, tenure, and other welfare problems, and helping local units plan their programs.

Official Journal: This organ was the official channel of communication of the Association.

Legislative: The major emphasis of the legislative program was selecting bills to be sponsored by the Association, participating in hearings on bills, interviewing legislative and state officials, and preparing information for the members.

Placement Bureau: This Bureau registered teachers on a list which employers could consult and notified teachers of vacancies. There was no charge to active members of the Association.

Public Relations: This included preparation of news releases, making speeches before lay groups, and interpreting the program of the Association to the public.

Research Services: The research activities were carried on by the executive secretary and the members of the Research Committee. The major activities were investigating teacher welfare problems, preparing reports for committees, supplying data for research studies, and publishing the findings.

Miscellaneous Services: This included any service not listed here. One of the most important was to aid lay groups which were seeking to better educational opportunities in the state.

Most of these services were not new, but in 1952 they were organized by the executive secretary to facilitate the administration of these services. They were also more widely publicized to encourage members to participate more actively in the program.

During Mr. Bowen's second year as president (1953–54), he presented his "Program of Emphasis" to the House of Delegates.[7] Most of his recommendations were restatements of programs already approved but needing special emphasis for further implementation. However, three new items were included:

1. The Committee on Tax Education and School Finance was asked to explore the possibility of free textbooks for schools.

2. Principals and physical education teachers should be employed on a year-round basis.

3. An increase of $5 per pupil for school construction was to be based on school enrollment.

A CHANGE IN NAME:
THE PALMETTO EDUCATION ASSOCIATION

Another change that occurred during the latter part of Mr. Bowen's administration was the name of the Association. The Constitution Committee of 1952, having J. R. Moorer and A. M. Anderson as co-chairmen, proposed a constitutional amendment that would change the name of the Association. The House of Delegates accepted the amendment and the name was changed to the Palmetto Education Association in 1953. Beginning with the first issue of 1954, the *Palmetto State Teachers Association Journal* became the *Palmetto Education Association Journal*.

1954–1956: TERM OF PRESIDENT HARPER

At its thirty-sixth Annual Convention held on April 1 and 2, 1954, new records were set by the Association. For the first time in the history of the Association, a lady, Dr. Madge Perry Harper,

John R. Bowen, principal of High Hill School in Spartanburg and Association president, 1952-54.

Dr. Madge Perry Harper, assistant director of instruction of the Orangeburg City Schools and PEA president, 1954-56.

assistant director of instruction of the Orangeburg City Schools, was elected president. Elected with her as vice-president was another lady, Mrs. Leila A. Bradby, instructor at Schofield School in Aiken. Both of these ladies along with the other officers assumed their duties July 1, 1954.

Another record broken in 1954 was in the area of memberships. An all-time high of 6,001 was reached, with an additional Palmetto Education Association—Future Teachers Association membership of 430. This was the fourth consecutive year that the membership had increased, but this marked the first time in the Association's history that the 6,000 membership figure was reached. As indicated at the beginning of this chapter, the previous high for memberships was 5,900 in March 1949. There was a decline in 1950 to 5,359 and then a slight increase in 1951 to 5,375. In 1952 there was another very slight increase. By 1953 the number increased to 5,841, not including 372 Future Teachers of America members. In April 1954 when the new membership record of 6,001 was reached, the 100 percent membership counties increased also, from two in 1952 to fourteen in 1954. The two counties reporting 100 percent membership in 1952 were Lee and Greenville Countys. Their presidents were N. G. Conyers of Lee and Mrs. Alberta T. Grimes of Greenville. The 14 counties with 100 percent membership in 1954 were Lee, Greenville, Oconee, Dorchester, Saluda, Cherokee, McCormick, Darlington, Hampton, Spartanburg, Pickens, Calhoun, Barnwell, and Abbeville.

Still another record broken at this convention was that the attendance was the largest in the history of the Association. The increase in the number of departments was the main reason for this wider interest in the affairs of the Palmetto Education Association.

As soon as Dr. Madge Harper assumed her duties as president, she immediately attempted to follow through on efforts of Mr. Bowen to get bids and funds to begin construction of the new Administrative Center. She declared a building emergency in her remarks to the House, asking that all assets of the Association be used in meeting this emergency. "However, the House of Delegates voted, after prolonged debate, to delay construction plans."[8] The Building Committee, which had previously obtained the services of architect J. H. Blanche of South Carolina State College to draw plans and specifications for the new home, made its first report to Mr. Bowen and several subsequent reports to the House of Delegates.

However, the House delayed approval until it could get a clear understanding of the financial capability of the Association to undertake a $75,000 project.

Although Dr. Harper was not successful in persuading the House of Delegates to begin construction of the new headquarters building, her administration may be credited with a number of achievements. Among them were the following:

1. A Council on Higher Education was organized. This organization was formed to provide an interest group for college teachers at the annual Palmetto Education Association convention, to create a publication or special bulletin that would come from the council dealing with problems of special interest to college teachers, and to serve as a clearing house for general problems common to all colleges in the state.

2. Two additional subject area groups were added to the 24 already organized. They were the Division of Pupil Personnel and Guidance with Jacob Tingman of Booker T. Washington High School in Columbia as president, and Special Education with Lutherine B. Smith as chairperson.

The Council on Higher Education of the Palmetto Education Association held its first meeting on November 19, 1954, at the the library of Benedict College. A planning session had been held at the request of Mr. Solomon during the last convention, and at that time Howard Jordan was appointed temporary chairman. At the November 19 meeting a permanent organization was formed with Mr. Jordan as elected chairman and Mrs. Helen A. Whiting as secretary.[9]

The membership in the Association increased from 6,001 in 1954 to 6,468 in April 1955. By March 1956, 6,718 of the 7,200 teachers were members of the Palmetto Education Association. In addition, 2,200 of these members joined the National Education Association and 1,700 were members of the American Teachers Association.

Dr. Harper was appointed by Governor Byrnes to represent South Carolina at the White House Conference on Education. She, along with G. A. Anderson, former president of the Association and an appointee of Governor Brynes, and Mr. Solomon were very active participants in the conference.

PEA STATEMENT OF PRINCIPLES

The Supreme Court's decision of 1954 and its implementation decree of 1955 met with deep resistance in South Carolina. The state legislature immediately appointed a School Segregation Committee with Senator Marion Gressette as chairman. The Committee invited organizations and individuals to meet with them.

The Palmetto Education Association requested an invitation to meet with the Committee. The PEA Executive Committee appointed a special committee to draft a "Statement of Principles." Upon approval of the Association's officers, the statement would be presented to the School Segregation Committee if invited. The invitation was received, and the special committee including President Madge P. Harper, Dr. Frank De Costa, Dr. T. B. Jones, and Executive Secretary W. E. Solomon who read the statement, appeared before the Committee.

Statement of Principles

The Palmetto Education Association has worked continuously over the past half century for the improvement of Education in South Carolina. Although it has been difficult at times to do so, the Association has held fast to the following beliefs:

1. The belief that it should sustain an abiding faith in democracy, not only as a form of government but as a way of life. Democracy in our on-going civilization is a growing and living concept, formulated to serve as a guide in the ever-increasing perplexities of life.

2. The belief that a basic tenet of democracy as a social philosophy is its emphasis on the worth and dignity of the individual in society. To this end, the early founders of the United States seemed determined to establish the individual as an entity. As a consequence of this tenet, laws of society— federal, state, and local—which degrade the individual because of such personal characteristics as color of skin, religion, and place of birth are inconsistent with this basic tenet of democracy. To the extent that any law—federal, state, or local—violates this tenet, to that extent is the segment of society which is governed by that law undemocratic.

3. The belief that a basic tenet of representative democracy is its emphasis on the respect for constitutional authority. Democracy grants every citizen the privilege of speech and the right to labor for and try to persuade others to accept the validity of his wishes. On the other hand, when the decision is made, the law-abiding citizen must conform to the laws which are passed. If this were not true, our society would become an anarchy, rather than a democracy.

4. The belief that the successful operation of democracy as a social philosophy is dependent upon a *universally* literate citizenry. This belief was held even by the early founders of the United States. Note the writings of Washington, Jefferson and Franklin.

5. The belief that a universally literate citizenry is attainable only through public support of education. Free public education and democracy in the United States have grown up together, and the public school is the creation of and the instrument for the democratic way of life. The wide differentials in individual incomes, the system of indirect taxation, and the importance of education to the preservation and improvement of the democratic society support this belief.

On the basis of these beliefs, the Palmetto Association is convinced:

1. That the recent ruling of the United States Supreme Court with respect to segregation in public education solely on the basis of race is consistent with the Association's beliefs No. 1 and No. 2.

2. That we, in South Carolina, cannot afford to formulate a plan of education which is inconsistent with the recent ruling of the United States Supreme Court. Such a plan would negate the tenet of democracy which is stated in the Association's belief No. 3. The schools under such a plan would become agencies of anarchy, rather than of democracy. The Association has consistently operated within the framework of constitutional laws and their interpretations.

3. That the Association is eager and feels obligated to cooperate with other agencies and individuals of the State in discussing, outlining, and implementing plans for universal public education in South Carolina within the framework of the recent ruling of the United States Supreme Court. This attitude of the Association is consistent with its beliefs No. 3, No. 4, and No. 5. To adopt a different attitude would be: (a) to ignore the values of universal public education; and (b) to tend to negate the principle of constitutional authority.[10]

PEA-SPONSORED HIGH SCHOOL ACTIVITIES

The South Carolina Secondary School Activities Association was organized in 1954 by the principals of the state to consolidate the activities of South Carolina high schools. These activities included football, basketball, baseball, music, forensics, student council, honor society, and clubs. This organization was sponsored by the Department of Secondary Schools Principals of the Palmetto Education Association.

The athletic program was supervised and organized by Robert E. Howard, principal of Wilkinson High School in Orangeburg. He divided the state of South Carolina into nine districts with three classifications, AAA, AA, and A. This enabled schools to compete on a more even basis.

The student council activities were headed by the founder of the student council programs in South Carolina, the Reverend William Parker, principal of Manning Training School in Manning, South Carolina. This organization held a two-day meeting each year to improve good citizenship and scholarship among the student councils throughout the state.

R. W. McGirt, principal of Emmett Scott High School in Rock Hill, was responsible for the music activities. He helped the organization sponsor interscholastic music activities of member schools. Noncompetitive district and state music festivals were held annually.

The forensic activities were headed by E. A. Finney, principal of Whittemore School in Conway. This group conducted oratoricals and debates between member institutions at the district and state level.

The honor society programs were headed by Dr. J. C. Parler, administrative principal of Orangeburg City Schools. It was designed to improve the level of scholarship among students in the state.

Each school paid dues of 20¢ per student. The funds were used to employ an executive secretary and underwrite other expenses of the organization. This organization was very successful and was supported by the principals because they recognized how necessary it was to consolidate and coordinate the activities of the high schools of the state.

1956–1958: DR. BRADBY SERVES AS PRESIDENT

The first classroom teacher to serve as president of the Palmetto Education Association was Dr. Leila A. Bradby, teacher of English and French at Schofield High School, Aiken, South Carolina. Before her election in 1956, she was vice-president with Dr. Harper from 1954 to 1956 and had served with distinction the three prior administrations at McCain, Potts, and Parler as secretary of the House of Delegates.

NEW ADMINISTRATIVE CENTER

In her first meeting with the House as president, she requested M. D. Bogan, chairman of the Building Committee, to make a report of the progress made on the construction plans for the new headquarters building. A more favorable climate was existing in October of 1956 for the acceptance of the report of the committee. The committee submitted the plans and specifications prepared by the architect, John Blanche, to contractors for bids, and the Langly Construction Company submitted a low bid of $60,454. The estimated cost was $75,000. The officers of the Association had earmarked $34,-246.15 for the project from membership, $455 from contributions,

Dr. Leila A. Bradby, instructor at Schofield High School in Aiken and PEA president, 1956-58.

and $3,246.15 from operating expenses. Since the membership was now close to 7,000 and $1 of every $5 was earmarked for the construction of the facility, the members of the House were convinced that the Association could anticipate approximately $7,000 a year to pay off the balance due. Consequently, the Building Committee's report was approved and construction began soon thereafter.

The dream of all the officers and members of the Palmetto Education Association, past and present, came true on Monday, September 9, 1957. On that date the Palmetto Education Association moved into its new Administrative Center. The building was a two-story, brick, fireproof, air-conditioned structure. It was designed to be income-producing by providing six offices upstairs to be rented. The office of the executive secretary, the office for secretaries, the records room, a conference room, a kitchenette, and rest rooms were located downstairs. This edifice was another indication of the professional spirit of the Palmetto Education Association members. It was indeed a great milestone in the history of the Association.

This modern two-story building was completed as the new headquarters for the Association in 1957. Constructed at a cost of $65,000, it provided housing for the administrative offices of the Association, a large lobby, lounge, kitchenette, conference rooms, and office space for additional income. Mortgage payments were completed in 1964. The Association occupied this building until merger with the South Carolina Education Association in 1968.

MEMBERS INCREASE PARTICIPATION

On December 15, 1956, 160 classroom teachers representing 40 county associations met at Allen University and organized the Palmetto Education Association Department of Classroom Teachers. In organizing this department these teachers carried out one of the long-standing objectives of the Association. It was felt that it would add strength and influence to our organization. H. L. Barksdale, who served the Association with distinction in numerous capacities, was elected president of this new department.

More than 400 teachers participated in Palmetto Education Association planning meetings. One was the Leadership Conference, which was instituted during the administration of J. C. Parler (1951) and an important feature in the program of the Palmetto Education Association since that time. The 1956 Conference was the best attended of all the conferences and strengthened the organization significantly. The other meeting was composed of presidents of county associations and chairpersons of the 16 standing committees. This meeting also had the best attendance since it had organized six years before. Of the 46 counties, 45 were represented.

The Palmetto Education Association participated in the National Education Association Centennial celebration. A special committee headed by Mrs. B. B. Sherrod was appointed by Dr. Bradby to make plans for the participation of the Palmetto Education Association.

The Natural Science Division of the Palmetto Education Association conducted its first Science Fair in April 1957. J. Michael Graves was chairman of the division when this fair was first held. James Green continued the project in 1958. Each high school and junior high school in the state was invited to participate through individual student projects and group projects. The young scientist who in the opinion of competent judges had the best project was given a trip to Los Angeles, California to participate in the National Science Fair. The first winner was Elma Sullivan of Wilkinson High School.

MEMBERSHIP CAMPAIGN

In 1957 Executive Secretary Solomon, as part of the special membership campaign launched in 1952, prepared a membership handbook which described all of the services of the state and national

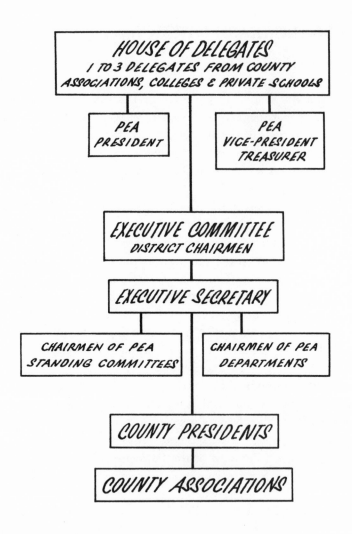

CHART 1. ORGANIZATION OF PEA,
1957 MEMBERSHIP HANDBOOK

organizations and established membership goals for 1957–58. The significant feature about this campaign was that the handbook proposed a plan for cooperative collection of dues. Guide sheets and report forms were provided those who were to collect dues in each county. This plan made it possible and desirable for each teacher to pay local Palmetto Education Association, National Education Association, and American Teachers Association dues by December 1. Since the Palmetto Education Association's program was expanding at such a rapid rate and the new Administration Center was constructed, there was an urgent need to increase its financial resources. The leadership felt that it was better to enlarge membership than raise the amount of the membership fee again. Another reason for the campaign was to raise the professional status of the Palmetto Education Association by increasing the number holding memberships in the National Education Association and the American Teachers Association. This campaign was very productive. The membership increased from 6,767 in 1957 to 7,181 in 1958. The number of 100 percent counties increased from 14 in 1954 to 27 in 1957, and 37 in 1958.

The Palmetto Education Association sponsored European tours for those teachers who desired to broaden their educational backgrounds.

1958–1960: PRESIDENT WILLIAMS SERVES

Following Dr. Bradby as president of the Palmetto Education Association was Allen Williams, principal of New Bethel School in Woodruff, South Carolina. Prior to his election to the presidency of the Palmetto Education Association, Mr. Williams served as president of the Spartanburg County Teachers Association and the Palmetto Education Association Department of County Presidents. While serving as the president of the Spartanburg County Teachers Association he was instrumental in obtaining 100 percent membership in the Palmetto Education Association. His ambition as the state Association president was to secure 100 percent membership in all schools in the state. Mr. Williams began his tenure of office on July 1, 1958.

The Association again elected a lady as vice-president. In 1958 Mrs. Alberta T. Grimes, guidance counselor at Sterling High School in Greenville and chairperson of the Palmetto Education Association Constitution Committee, was elected vice-president.

One of the most commendable attributes of the presidents of the Palmetto Education Association was their ability to meet the urgent and specific needs of the Association during their respective terms of office. They knew where to place the emphasis at the stage of the Association's development that they administered. Mr. Bowen described the program he presented to the House of Delegates as a "Program of Emphasis." Fortunately for the Palmetto Education Association, Mr. Williams demonstrated this same ability. Like his predecessors before him he conferred many times with the past presidents between the date of his election and the date his tenure of office began. He studied the organizational structure and the operational procedures and found them to be adequate for the present. However, he discovered that there was a considerable amount of information about the Palmetto Education Association that the members did not have. The Association had grown so rapidly that the membership could not keep up with the forward movement. Consequently, he immediately focused his attention upon informing the constituents about the program of the organization:

> I was determined that ere my tenure ends, every teacher in the state would have access to information pertaining to all phases of the Association's program directly through participation, or indirectly through representation.[11]

HANDBOOK OF ASSOCIATION INFORMATION

To accomplish this purpose Mr. Williams requested Executive Secretary Solomon to compile all pertinent information about the Association and prepare an information handbook to be given to all persons in leadership positions. The title of the publication published in November 1959 was *Organized For Action.* The first paragraph of the foreword follows:

> This handbook represents fifty years of thinking and planning by members of our Association. During these years many changes were made in attempts to perfect a pattern of organization that would give opportunity for maximum participation and representation in the deliberations of the Association. In recent years our pattern of organization has enabled us to reach directly, or indirectly, through service, membership, participation, and representation an unbelievable percentage of our potential.[12]

The booklet contained 63 pages and included information about the following:

1. The organization, services, and policies of the Palmetto Education Association

2. The organization of county associations

3. The services of the Palmetto Education Association, National Education Association, and the American Teachers Association

4. The Department of Classroom Teachers

5. The Palmetto Student Education Association

6. The Palmetto Education Association standing committees and a list of their duties, including the District and County Committees

7. Membership goals by counties and districts

8. An appendix with a directory of Palmetto Education Association officers, district officers, the Executive Committee, county presidents, Classroom Teacher presidents, departmental chairpersons, Palmetto Education Association standing committees, and the House of Delegates.

Allen Williams, principal of New Bethel School in Woodruff and PEA president, 1958-60.

PARTICIPATION IN NEA BY PEA MEMBERS

Mr. Williams also designated certain members to attend meetings of the National Education Association commissions, committees, and departments. He told these appointees that he expected to use them in similar positions in the Palmetto Education Association program. Therefore, he urged not only attendance but participation in the deliberations of these meetings. In one month's time 62 members participated in national meetings. This was a record for the Association.

FURTHER ACHIEVEMENTS

An executive secretary was employed by the Board of Control of the South Carolina Secondary School Activities Association. John L. McCoy began his tenure of service in September 1958. The officers of the SCSSAA were Dr. Gerard Anderson, president; Aaron Rucker, vice-president; and C. C. Woodson, secretary-treasurer.

Memberships continued to increase. They rose from 7,181 in 1958 to 7,386 in 1959. At the end of Mr. Williams' term on May 1, 1960, the number rose to 7,700, which was 98 percent of all Negro teachers in the state.

A Teacher Education and Professional Standards Commission was organized by the Palmetto Education Association. Dr. Howard Jordan was elected chairman.

The Palmetto Science Fair Committee received a contribution of $300 from the Palmetto Medical, Dental, and Pharmaceutical Association to pay the travel expenses of the first- and second-place winners of the Science Fair held in 1959 to attend the National Science Fair in Hartford, Connecticut. A committee of doctors, C. O. Spann, F. J. Jenkins, and H. E. Caldwell, was appointed by the medical association to study the possibility of making the Science Fair one of its annual projects.

However, this support of the project by the Palmetto Medical, Dental, and Pharmaceutical Association discontinued after one year, and the North Carolina Mutual Life Insurance Company and South Carolina State College made contributions to the Science Fair.

Both Mr. Williams and Mr. Solomon made special trips to Washington, D.C. to lobby for federal aid to education bills. Their principal contacts were with the South Carolina congressional delegation.

CHAPTER VI

1960-1967: Improving Teacher Competencies and Student Performance

Use your gifts faithfully, and they shall be enlarged; Practice what you know, and you shall attain to higher knowledge.

Matthew Arnold

With the election of Mrs. Alberta T. Grimes to the presidency in April 1960, the Palmetto Education Association entered a new decade. The theme for 1960–61 was "Excellence in Education for a Decade of Decision in the 1960's." The Association was on the threshold of the third phase of its long-range program. During the previous decade of the fifties, two stages had been completed. The first stage began with the Leadership Conferences, which enabled the development of a strong organizational structure uniting the counties and districts with the state organization and at the same time the adoption of the successful features of the National Education Association. The second stage of development began with the Planning Conferences, which provided opportunities for wide participation of the members in the affairs of the Association. Following these conferences special provisions were made to keep all members informed of all the aspects of the expanding and service oriented program.

1960–1962: GOALS SET BY PRESIDENT GRIMES

In this new decade of the sixties the Palmetto Education Association entered a third stage, prepared to concentrate upon the improvement of teacher competencies and student performance. Mrs. Grimes was highly qualified to provide the leadership for the new thrust. She previously served as classroom teacher, guidance counselor, and dean of students and held many leadership positions in the Palmetto Education Association, National Education Association, and the American Teachers Association. In her first message to the membership she made this statement: "We will need to develop goals within our Association which will facilitate an educational program geared to the dynamic changes in today's world."[1]

A list of Educational Goals for South Carolina was prepared by Executive Secretary Solomon and submitted to the House of Delegates for the consideration of its members. The list was adopted by the House in November 1961. Part I focused upon the pupil, and Part II concerned the teacher.

Educational Goals for South Carolina—Part I

I. *Compulsory School Attendance Law:* A compulsory school attendance law for all children and youth between the ages of five through eighteen. The Voting Rights Act enables all individuals of proper age to register and vote in elections. Industry needs a literate labor force. These two reasons, and others, supplement our belief that the State should adopt a compulsory school attendance law.

II. *School Systems Should Operate on the K–12 Plan:* The Headstart experiences enjoyed by students and the summer experimental programs conducted by a few districts supported the need for pre-school experiences for all children. The high percentage of parents with less than five years of educational training makes a kindergarten experience a must for our schools. We pledge support to all school systems in the organization and administration of Headstart projects with the hope that these will lead to the kindergarten program.

III. *Reduction in Pupil–Teacher Ratio:* It is difficult to determine a pupil–teacher ratio for South Carolina schools. Many schools with high enrollments have a number of classes with forty or more students. Our Association supports a lower pupil–teacher ratio in the elementary schools. Twenty-five to one will enable the teacher to give time for individualized instruction. An average of 22.5 should be the ratio in the secondary schools. (Federal funds can be obtained for special projects with small groups of students. We urge school systems to initiate these projects.)

IV. *The State Should Provide Free Textbooks:* Many families are not able to pay the rental fee on textbooks. Federal funds can be used to obtain textbooks for children whose parents' income is within the poverty range. Parents of many other children are not far above this poverty figure. Therefore, we request that our State begin now to provide free textbooks for all grades. We commend those school districts that are providing free textbooks for elementary and high schools.

V. *Supervising Principals:* A school with ten or more teachers should have a principal free of classroom duties. The principal, in addition to administrative duties, must supervise classroom instruction.

VI. *Supervisors and School Specialists:* Supervisors of instruction and school specialists should be employed in all school districts. Adequate supervision improves the quality of instruction. The school specialists complement the work of supervisors and teachers. Specialists in reading and counseling are our greatest need.

VII. *Equipment and Instructional Supplies:* The school must have modern equipment and instructional supplies in sufficient quantity. Students should have the opportunity of using equipment needed in a class exercise.

Educational Goals for South Carolina—Part II

I. *State Aid Salary Schedule:* The average salary of teachers in the nation is the goal we suggest for our State aid salary. Salary increases leading toward this goal will permit superintendents and principals to employ the best graduates of South Carolina colleges and recruit the best graduates from out-of-state colleges. We support a 20 percent increase for all teachers in the 1961–62 salary schedule.

II. *Tenure Law:* A tenure law that gives some promise of security. Teachers must have administrative approval of their work. This will aid them in their efforts to obtain the status they deserve from the society which charges them with the responsibility of developing responsible citizens.

III. *Teacher Retirement:* We advocate increasing the present benefits to a minimum of $100,000. We also support the discontinuance of the discriminatory practice that exists in benefits received by those persons retiring between 1957 and 1963. The increase in cost of living makes retirement benefits a major consideration in the selection of a position.

IV. *Clerical Help:* Secretarial and clerical help in all schools will relieve teachers of these duties.

V. *Additional Visiting Teachers:* The employment of an additional visiting teacher in each county. The rapid increase in our school age population makes this a necessity.[2]

Mrs. Grimes invited speakers for the general sessions who had some expertise in improving instruction and raising achievement levels of pupils. This was especially true of Dr. Aaron Brown, project director of the Phelps–Stokes Fund. The programs of the departments and the student education associations supplemented the general sessions with research projects and small conference sessions. In addition, teachers were reminded of their responsibility for improving their instructional competencies. The combined efforts of the individual teacher and the educational association were required to get the best results.

In October 1961 the Palmetto Education Association sponsored the first annual conference on the improvement of instruction.

Membership reached an all time high during Mrs. Grimes' tenure. In April 1961 the number increased from 7,700 in 1960 to 8,066. In 1962 the number rose to 8,100. These membership increases were even more remarkable since the fee was increased from $5.00 to $7.50 in 1961. Thirty-nine of forty-six counties were 100 percent, and the National Education Association membership among Palmetto Education Association members was 3,829 in 1961. The

Mrs. Alberta T. Grimes, counselor at Sterling High School in Greenville and PEA president, 1960-62.

Hudson L. Barksdale of Mary H. Wright Elementary School in Spartanburg and PEA president, 1962-64.

American Teachers Association memberships rose to 3,939. The president had requested 4,000 in each.

Three departments were added in 1961–62 to those already organized. They were in the areas of Adult Education, Foreign Languages, and Art.

Reports from the National Commission on Teacher Education and Professional Standards (TEPS) of the National Education Association and sponsors of Student National Education chapters and Future Teachers of America Clubs indicate that the Palmetto Education Association had the largest number of members among those states which had two associations.[3] The teachers responsible for this good record were Miss Trudelle W. Wimbush and Mrs. Alberta Grimes. It is an indication of their interest in our youth.

During Mrs. Grimes' administration a General Culture Seminar for teachers was begun. This project was designed to prepare teachers to improve their scores on the National Teachers Examination. Mr. Solomon assumed the leadership in the implementation of the project.

During this same period the Palmetto Education Association made a strong effort to sponsor Headstart programs in South Carolina when the state Department of Education and the state legislature would not take the initiative in the sponsorship because of the non-discrimination policies. Mrs. Grimes, Mr. Solomon, and other interested Association members invited Mrs. Greenberg, the national director of Headstart, to South Carolina to discuss the possibility of organizing Headstart programs in South Carolina. The first community-sponsored project was started in the city of Greenville, and the first college-sponsored project was begun at Voorhees College in Denmark. According to Mr. Solomon, "those efforts of the Palmetto Education Association to sponsor Headstart Programs brought about a change in the attitude of the State Legislature and the State Department of Education." After some delay these programs were sponsored by the state Department of Education.

1962–1964: NEW PRESIDENT BARKSDALE

Just as Mrs. Grimes educational experiences equipped her to provide the leadership that the third stage of the Palmetto Education Association's development required, Hudson L. Barksdale, who was elected president in 1962, had the necessary credentials to continue the attainment of the educational goals of this stage. At this particular period in its history the Association needed leaders who had both training and experience in improving instruction and raising student achievement levels. Mrs. Grimes' experiences as a classroom teacher and a summer school instructor of teachers were very helpful. Mr. Barksdale was elected "Spartanburg County Teacher of the Year" in 1954, and as president of the Palmetto Education Association Department of Classroom Teachers he represented that department at three National Classroom Teacher Conferences and two regional meetings. He was highly qualified for the special emphasis of the Association at the time of his election.

To continue the forward movement in the areas of teacher competence and pupil achievement, Mr. Barksdale, with the cooperation of the other officers, committees, commissions, and volunteers, increased the number of workshops for professional improvement in these two areas and also started a project for teaching the culturally deprived.

Contributors to the *Palmetto Education Association Journal* were encouraged to prepare papers and do research in the areas of teacher competence and pupil performance. Between 1962 and 1964 many articles were published dealing with the academically talented pupil, quality education, improving communication skills, helping underachievers, recent trends in teaching, and characteristics of a good teacher.

On November 10, 1962, the policy-making body adopted the following program for the Association to pursue for the next year:

Attendance Laws. South Carolina cannot meet the labor demands of new and expanding industries unless school attendance is compulsory. We cannot expect to train people for technical jobs when their educational training is below the eighth grade level.

A study of the 1961 graduating classes in schools for Negro children revealed that five out of six enrolled in the first grade in 1949 dropped out of school before graduation, and only 16 percent of the graduates entered college in the fall of 1961. A high percentage of South Carolina youth continue to fail the Selective Service Registrant Mental Test. In 1960, 54.4 percent failed the test.

Reduction in Teacher Load. According to our studies there are too many students enrolled per teacher employed in our schools. Last year 387 classes had more than 40 students enrolled. There is a legislative proposal to employ teachers on an ADA of 30 students. This will reduce the teacher load, but in the absence of an attendance law, and with only one visiting teacher in 42 counties, it will create a tremendous problem for our teachers. Consolidated schools make home visitations a financial burden.

Teaching Principals. We support a legislative proposal to employ, with state aid, one additional person for every twenty teachers employed in a school district. We hope the additional person will replace the teaching principal. This will free him to properly supervise the instructional program and perform the administrative work of the position.

An Expenditure of $210 Per Pupil. We support the state superintendent's proposed equalization fund. This fund will supplement the per pupil expenditure in counties spending less than $210. This will represent a minimum per pupil expenditure for the school districts.

State Aid Salary. We advocate a 15 percent increase in the present state aid salary schedule. We need it to compete with our neighboring states. We need it to hold our better teachers who are lured away each year by salary offers ranging from $600 to $2,000 more than their present salary. An attractive state aid salary schedule will permit our superintendents and principals to recruit better graduates from out of state colleges and to supplement our own college graduates.

Equal Supplements to State Aid Salary. The school districts supplement from local funds the state aid salaries of teachers employed. Some districts do not supplement state aid salaries of teachers in schools for Negro children. Other districts do not pay an equal supplement based on training and experience. A district supplement in equal sums based on training and experience would help us retain our best college graduates and experienced teachers.

Tenure for Teachers. Tenure is an employment status gained after two or three years of teaching in the same school system. It indicates the School Board is satisfied with the teacher's performance. This form of professional approval gives added status to the profession and should meet public approval.

Teacher Retirement. The cost of living index continues to rise. This increase in living expenses makes it difficult for retired teachers to maintain their positions of service in community organizations. Present minimum benefits of $70 and $80 should be increased to $100.[4]

Some of the goals were the same as those adopted in 1961 during the administration of Mrs. Grimes. However, they were restated because they were only partially attained or not reached at all.

To implement this program the Executive Committee instructed Mr. Solomon to plan a special conference during the month of January 1963. There was a growing concern about the "drop out" problem and the increasing number of teachers leaving the state each year for better salaries and conditions of work.

When the House of Delegates adopted the Legislative Program for the Association, it gave approval to requests for meetings of legislative committee chairpersons and lay people from each county in the state. The executive secretary arranged for a meeting of county presidents on January 5, 1964. These presidents were asked to submit the names of the chairperson of their legislative committees and four lay persons from their counties. Correspondence was then sent to them inviting the chairpersons to a meeting on January 12 and the lay persons on January 23. All but eight counties responded. The purpose of these meetings was to get the full cooperation of all county presidents, county legislative committees, and influential lay people throughout the state in helping the Palmetto Education Association achieve its legislative program.

Mr. Barksdale had some goals which he referred to as "additional" to those mandated by the House of Delegates. Among the most important were the following:

1. Achieve 100 percent membership in the Palmetto Education Association.

2. Attain at least 50 percent membership in the National Education Association.

3. Increase attendance at the annual conventions.

4. Complete payment for the headquarters building.

5. Increase dues to $10.00.

6. Increase staff at Palmetto Education Association headquarters.

Mr. Barksdale was successful in realizing all of these "additional" goals except the 100 percent membership in the Palmetto Education Association. However, the membership rose from 8,100 in 1962, to 8,430 in 1963, and 8,429 in 1964. The amazing feature of this increase was that it was achieved after the House of Delegates voted to raise dues from $7.50 to $10.00. This was the second increase in four years. The Association surpassed its previous records and achieved a new high in Palmetto Education Association and American Teachers Association memberships. In 1964, the National Education Association memberships increased to 4,565 and the American Teachers

Former presidents of the Association received special awards during Mr. Barksdale's administration. *Standing left to right:* J. T. W. Mims (1942-44), G. A. Anderson (1938-40), J. R. Bowen (1952-54), Allen Williams (1958-60), and John F. Potts (1948-50). *Seated left to right:* Dr. Leila Bradby (1956-58), Dr. Madge P. Harper (1954-56), Dr. C. A. Johnson (1930-32), and Mrs. Alberta T. Grimes (1960-62).

Association to 4,311. This was more than 50 percent since the total number of teachers in Negro schools that year was 8,667.

Other evidence of progress during Mr. Barksdale's tenure was the election of a Board of Trustees to exercise general oversight of the Administrative Center and a Welfare Administration Board to administer the Teacher Welfare Program. The House of Delegates earmarked $1.25 of each $10.00 membership for Teacher Welfare. A bookkeeper was added to the headquarters staff, and provision was made to provide an assistant to Mr. Solomon.

1964–1966: C. E. WATKINS, SUCCESSOR TO PRESIDENCY

When Mr. Barksdale's term expired, Clarence E. Watkins, the vice-president, was elected to succeed him in 1964. This procedure of elevating the vice-president to the presidency was not required by the constitution, but it was followed in most of the elections of the Association. The rationale for this action was the desire for continuity of efforts to attain Association goals. With two years of experience as vice-president the incumbent was better qualified to keep the Association constantly moving forward. Mr. Watkins, who was supervising principal of the Wateree Elementary School in Camden, also had served as president of the Kershaw County Teachers Association and chairman of the department of principals of that county association. Under his leadership both groups attained and maintained 100 percent membership in the county association, the Fifth Congressional District, the Palmetto Education Association, the American Teachers Association, and the National Education Association.

Like his predecessors Mr. Watkins gave priority to the on-going program of the Palmetto Education Association. Special attention was given the two goals established during Mrs. Grimes' administration and partially implemented during the presidency of Mr. Barksdale—teacher competence and pupil achievement. The theme "Teacher Competence in an Automated Society" was more widely used. In his first message to the membership Mr. Watkins stated:

> Education is our business. The improvement of working conditions for our teachers, and better learning situations for the children and youth of our state are "Items of importance" to us in the Palmetto Education Association. With this thought in mind, we have attempted to sponsor workshops, and instructional meetings on all

levels. We have stressed these activities in the various subject area fields. The attendance and participation in these activities have been very encouraging. We must continue these kinds of events if we are going to improve teacher competence in this everchanging society.[5]

The educational goals adopted and mandated by the House of Delegates in 1961 were re-studied and re-stated annually by the House of Delegates. Reference has already been made of the Association's program in 1962. There were very few changes in the goals between 1961 and 1966. All of the adopted programs included a compulsory school attendance law, school systems operating from kindergarten to 12 grades, a reduction in pupil-teacher ratio, free textbooks, principals free of teaching duties, school specialists, modern equipment, and more instructional supplies. For teachers the program included a 20 percent increase in salaries, equal supplements to state aid salaries, a tenure law, and higher retirements benefits. One item added after 1961 was an expenditure of $210 per pupil. Another was representation of a cross section of the state's population on the state, county, and district school boards.

Clarence E. Watkins, principal of Wateree Elementary School in Camden and PEA president, 1964-66.

119

After these goals were adopted by the House of Delegates, the Executive Committee and the Legislative Committee of the Palmetto Education Association called a meeting of presidents of county associations and chairpersons of legislative committees of these county associations for the purpose of seeking effective ways of attaining these goals. Following this meeting, a conference of lay people from each county was held to discuss the role of the layperson in the implementation of the Association's goals.

During the administration of Mr. Watkins some of the goals were partially realized. A few districts provided free textbooks, a compulsory school attendance bill was introduced in the legislature, and modern equipment and more instructional materials were provided. Mr. Watkins made the following remarks:

> . . . our efforts to get a tenure bill introduced and an amendment that would increase the number of persons on the State Board of Education had good support from two of the state's top lobbyists.
>
> Our proposed increase to the State Aid salary schedule did not look good. We were almost certain that we would get an increase in the State Aid schedule, but our 20 percent increase request has not excited our legislative committee members in County associations enough to make them go all out in their efforts to obtain support.[6]

In addition to giving priority to the attainment of the Association goals, Mr. Watkins completed a project begun during Mr. Barksdale's administration—the reorganization of the Teacher Defense Fund. The Executive Committee formulated a set of proposed rules for governing the Palmetto Education Association Defense Welfare Fund (the House of Delegates changed the name from Palmetto Education Association Welfare Fund). More specific information may be found in Chapter XIII.

CHAPTER VII

Meeting the Challenge of Change

Today is not yesterday. We ourselves change. How then, can our works and thoughts if they are always to be the fittest, continue always the same.

Thomas Carlyle

It was during Mr. Watkins' term of office that the Association took its first step toward unification with the South Carolina Education Association. During the summer of 1964 at its Seattle Convention, the National Education Association "adopted a resolution requesting the teacher associations in 11 southern states to draft a plan of merger by July 1, 1966."[1] The resolution specified 11 states because white associations in 6 of the 17 states with two associations voluntarily opened their membership to Negroes following the historic decision of the United States Supreme Court on May 17, 1954 invalidating segregation. The six states were Delaware, the District of Columbia, Kentucky, Maryland, Oklahoma, and West Virginia. The eleven states involved in the resolution were Alabama, Arkansas, Florida, Georgia, Louisiana, Mississippi, North Carolina, Tennessee, Texas, Virginia, and the state of South Carolina. Florida and Texas had already made some progress toward unification before the resolution was adopted. However, the other nine states did not report any jointly approved plans to the National Education Association's Executive Committee.

The departments affiliated with the National Education Association were requested to begin merger discussions. In South Carolina, the Department of Elementary School Principals and the Department of Secondary School Principals received invitations from the

121

National Education Association to explore merger possibilities. However, it was agreed by the officers in both groups that these departments would wait until the state associations completed their jointly approved plans.

BEGINNING OF THE UNIFICATION OF STATE ASSOCIATIONS

The Palmetto Education Association took immediate action on this resolution, and an ad hoc committee drafted guidelines which were presented to the House of Delegates on October 31, 1964. The House adopted the guidelines and approved a procedure for unification which the committee presented. In addition, this policy-making body instructed the Executive Committee to implement the plans and procedures. The Executive Committee very wisely submitted copies of these principles and procedures to each county association and had them published in the *Palmetto Education Association Journal*. In addition, they were discussed in detail at a Leadership Conference held on May 1, 1965. The delegates representing county associations were urged to delay efforts for unification at the county level until the two state teacher associations reached an agreement.

Because of the great significance of this document, it is presented in its entirety.

Principles and Procedures Covering the Unification of State Teachers Associations

The Palmetto Education Association believes that the principle of equal opportunities for all people, without regard to race, creed, or color, should govern the organization and functioning of the teaching profession, and of professional associations wherever the profession exists. We will, through our association's program, endeavor to facilitate the achievement of this end.

This has particular relevance in our state where dual associations now exist. True unity and integration of the profession can be achieved only through the cooperative efforts and mutual interaction of the two existing associations. Unilateral action will only serve to produce needless tensions, antagonisms and suspicions. Joint and cooperative action will be productive of harmony, mutual respect, and above all, understanding.

I. *Basic Principles:* Certain basic principles must be established to guide the two associations in the establishment of procedures for unification. The following principles shall serve this purpose.

A. Neither association shall expect or insist that the other association should agree to its abolition merely to have its members enter the remaining association on an individual basis. They should not expect, solicit nor insist on the above provisions on a district or county level.

B. The uniting and consolidation of the associations and of the profession can be achieved effectively only through negotiations at the highest level by the leaders of the two associations. Basic principles governing such unification must be jointly and mutually determined at the state level. Districts and counties should seek, subscribe and adhere to the state policies and procedures.

C. The removal of the racially restrictive provisions from a state association's constitution is an important step toward unity and consolidation, but only a first step. It creates the legally permissible framework without which unity is impossible.

D. Local option can be most effective only where there is a specific common policy at the state level that can give guidance and direction to local associations. Such common policies at the state level should be established before any action is taken by local associations. In cases where local associations have already acted, two steps should be taken:

1. Cessation of unification at the local level until there is an established common policy at the state level.

2. Require all locals to conform to this established state policy, whether they are unified prior to, or after, the adoption of the state policy.

II. *Procedures:* Certain minimum procedures would seem to be necessary if unification is to be accomplished with a minimum of friction, a maximum of understanding, and with reasonable consensus.

A. A joint steering committee composed of optimum representation from each of the two associations should be established. This committee should be assigned the task of devising principles and procedures for joint action toward unification of the two associations. Such principles and procedures should include the following:

1. A study of the program and services of each association by a joint committee. The committee should draft recommendations of programs and services for the unified association. The recommendations should be submitted to each association for approval.

2. An inventory of equipment, furniture, and capital investment by a joint committee. The complete inventory should be published in organs of the associations.

3. Arrange for the drafting of a new constitution by a joint constitution committee. The constitution should incorporate essential principles of the constitutions of the two existing associations.

4. All standing and other essential committees traditional in each separate association should be continued and reorganized as standing

committees of the new association.

5. All committees should be composed of an equal number of members from each separate association during the interim while plans for unification of the two associations are being devised.

B. Continued representation at the national level is important for all members of the profession. Any plan for unification should provide for fair representation in the National Education Association on the part of the members of both previous associations. In this connection:

1. Our state qualifies for only one NEA Director. We feel that the directorship should rotate until we qualify for a second director.

2. When our state qualifies for more than one NEA Director, each former association shall have representation.

3. Recommendations to NEA staff for appointments to NEA Commissions or Committees shall include members of former associations.

4. Provisions shall be established whereby a state's delegation to the NEA convention shall be composed of members of both former separate associations roughly in proportion to the membership of each.

C. In Item I above, mention was made of the need for a common policy on unification at the state level and for certain basic principles to govern unification. The following principles shall apply:

1. A time limit shall be set during which progressive steps toward unification shall be taken. The date for final consummation of unification shall be jointly determined.

2. In the initial stages the Board of Directors of the separate associations shall meet in joint session and shall serve as the initial Unified Board of Directors.

3. The Board of Directors of the unified association shall be constituted from the membership of the Boards of the two separate associations and representation on the unified Board of Directors shall be in proportion to the membership of the two separate associations.

4. Members of both original associations shall have an equal opportunity to serve in all positions of the unified association. Provisions assuring this equality of opportunity, especially in the initial stages, shall be established.

5. Membership on all commissions, committees, and other bodies of the association shall be generally in proportion to the memberships of the two original associations.

6. The staffs and office personnel of the two separate associations shall be retained in the unification; and positions and salaries in the unified association shall be determined on the basis of training, experience, efficiency, and present position.

D. Consolidation at the local levels shall be consistent with the policies, principles and procedures adopted at the state level.

1. Maximum use will be made of joint consultative committees, human relations and other type conferences and workshops to facilitate unification at the local level.

2. In the initial stages, to break down existing barriers and to facilitate communication and understanding, local affiliates of the two original associations will be assisted in the holding of joint meetings, workshops, seminars, and inter-group and human relations conferences.

3. Unification at the local level will be governed by the time table established at the state level unless exceptions are mutually agreed to at the state level.

III. *Concluding Statement:* Complete and permanent unification shall be considered effected only after all basic issues involving the particular interests of the two original associations have been mutually resolved. Only in this way can reasonable unity of purpose and action be assured. The unified association shall adopt, as policy, and work toward the implementation of the principle of the employment of teaching personnel at all levels in the public schools of the state based on training, experience, and satisfaction of state certification requirements.

The unified association will, moreover, urge the adoption, by the state and by local school boards, an open door policy for the attendance of all schools by all children without regard to race, creed or color. When this is accomplished, there will be no more "Negro schools" and "white schools." There will be only "schools," attended by "pupils," staffed by "teachers" and administered by "administrators." [2]

Before any final decisions were made, the Executive Committee wanted to make certain that the county association membership had discussed and understood the merger plan and had an opportunity to offer suggestions and recommendations for improvement.

On October 30, 1965, Mr. Barksdale, chairman of the Unification Committee, made a report on unification to the House of Delegates. After giving a brief history of how the committee originated, he stated that "its purpose was to prepare plans, on which we could meet as equals of SCEA, discuss unification, and work together to formulate the joint plans as requested by the NEA." [3]

He also informed the body that the presidents and executive secretaries of the Palmetto Education Association and the South Carolina Education Association had met and made the following recommendations:

1. SCEA will make efforts to get their local associations to wait until plans are completed at the state level.

2. SCEA will appoint a committee to meet with the PEA committee.

3. All legal matters are to be handled by competent attorneys.

4. Efforts will be made to prevent SCEA from raiding PEA members.

A committee composed of Mr. Barksdale, President Watkins, W. E. Solomon, Mrs. Ellen Watson, and John F. Potts was appointed to work jointly with its SCEA counterpart.

It was pointed out by Mr. Barksdale that both associations had publicly announced their willingness and readiness to unify. However, he expressed the strong desire of the Palmetto Education Association Unification Committee to hold fast to Palmetto Education Association because of the need to negotiate from strength.

Additional progress made toward uniting the two associations will be discussed when the administration of Mrs. Ellen Watson is described.

It is interesting to note that the discussion of unification affected the steady growth of membership during 1966–67. After reaching an all time high of 8,630 members in 1965, there was a slight decrease in membership in 1966 to 8,588. While the Palmetto Education Association memberships were decreasing, the National Education Association memberships of the Palmetto Education Association increased. In 1966 the NEA memberships reached a total of 5,626 and in 1967 climbed to 6,338. The reason for these membership changes was the growing belief among PEA members that their Association would eventually merge with the South Carolina Education Association and that the only professional teachers' organization they could depend on to provide the needed services and protection to teachers would be the National Education Association. However,

PEA leaders made a strong effort to keep the Association strong and viable until unification became a reality. As a result of these efforts the enrollment rose to 8,618 in 1967.

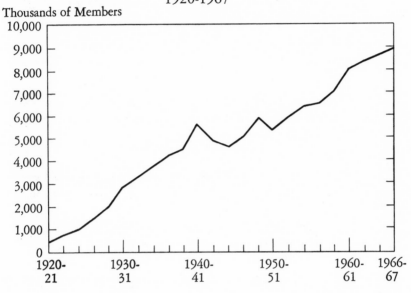

MEMBERSHIP GROWTH OF THE PEA
1920-1967

CHART 2.

1966: ELECTION OF LAST PEA PRESIDENT, ELLEN C. WATSON

Mrs. Ellen C. Watson became the fourth woman to be elected president of the Association since 1954. Her tenure of office began May 1, 1966 and ended on April 1, 1967 when the Palmetto Education Association and the South Carolina Education Association were merged. In addition to the experience she received while serving as vice-president for two years, Mrs. Watson served as president of the Spartanburg County Teachers Association, chairperson of the Fourth Congressional District, state membership chairperson, and a member of the Unification Committee.

127

President Watson had hoped to continue to reach the goals outlined in the Legislative Committee report to the House of Delegates on November 5, 1966. However, the pressures associated with unification were so demanding that most of her attention during her one-year term of office was devoted to merging the two organizations. According to Mrs. Watson, her administration was divided into two phases:

> Our first objective was to hold together solidly until a real merger plan could be worked out. Through great effort on the part of many persons this was accomplished in a creditable manner . . . .
>
> Then came the second phase: the formulation of a merger plan. This was the soul searching and sometimes agonizing part of the program, but it had to be done.
>
> After many hours, days, weeks and several months a plan was produced. This "skeleton" needed the "flesh" of interpretation and explanation before it could be accepted. After this was added, the acceptance came.[4]

UNIFICATION PREPARATION

On November 5, 1966 Mr. Barksdale, chairman of the PEA Unification Committee, made a report to the House of Delegates. He stated that the Association had three committees at work on the

Mrs. Ellen C. Watson of Carver High School in Spartanburg and PEA president, 1966-67.

problem of unification, a contact committee of six persons, the unification committee of seven persons, and sub-committees working on various aspects of the problem. Four meetings were held with the committee appointed by the South Carolina Education Association to prepare a joint statement to be submitted to the National Education Association Executive Committee. In addition, two meetings were held with sub-committees working on areas of Programs and Services, Assets and Liabilities, Local Associations, Organizational Structure, Personnel, and Legal Aspects. These committees were requested to complete their work by January 1, 1967.

Mr. Barksdale also reported that the National Education Association requested a meeting in Columbia with the presidents and presidents-elect of both organizations and with the joint committee of the Palmetto Education Association and the South Carolina Education Association on November 12 at the University of South Carolina. Topics for discussion were a timetable for merger steps to be taken, and organizational structure to be established.

It was pointed out by Mr. Barksdale that the Palmetto Education Association had done some things for its members that the South Carolina Education Association was not set up to do. He gave as examples the welfare cases and the Rackley and Clarendon County cases. The Palmetto Education Association protected the rights of Negro teachers.[5]

DRAFTING OF MERGER PLANS

It was March 4, 1967 before the House of Delegates assembled to vote on unification. President Watson appointed a committee consisting of Isaac White, E. M. Henry, Claudius Conner, and James F. Moorer to take charge of the voting on the proposed plan of merger. The members of the Unification Committee were present to answer any questions and clarify statements. Copies of the proposed merger plan were sent to each member prior to the meeting.

After a lengthy discussion and questions about the voting procedure, it was decided that the voting would be done by roll call and secret ballot. The results of the voting revealed that 54 members voted against the proposed merger plan and 48 voted for it.

The NEA director for South Carolina, Miss Gladys Robinson, asked members of the two committees to meet to discuss objections of the PEA members to the merger plan. The committees met in the school of education at the University of South Carolina. The PEA members were asked if they had the authority to make decisions. W. E. Solomon stated he thought their committee should report to the full original committee of 12 to obtain information and then meet with the SCEA committee. Other members of the PEA committee disagreed and caucused at the request of Mrs. Watson. After the caucus, the PEA committee stated they had the authority to make decisions. The SCEA members expressed the opinion that it was not necessary to continue the meeting because the PEA committee had previously adopted the plan. The meeting adjourned.

In a meeting in Atlanta on March 21, the acting executive secretary of NEA, Alan West, asked W. E. Solomon, PEA executive secretary, to discuss the present state of merger. Solomon told Mr. West the PEA committee did not get any of their proposals adopted even though committee representation was equal. The vote on issues, he said, was always 7–5 and in a few instances 8–4. There was never a 6–6 vote. Solomon expressed concern over the drafting and ratification of the constitution, the positions his staff would have in the new association, and the protection of PEA members. He wanted their contributions to the NAACP Legal Defense and Educational Fund continued and their Defense Welfare Fund kept intact.

A memorandum of agreement was drafted, and Mr. West assured Mr. Solomon that NEA would support his concerns. Solomon expressed doubt about NEA support because he and others had been trying to get NEA to draft guidelines for merger. However, Mr. Solomon agreed to the following plan:

1. Jim Williams, NEA Southeast director, would become a party to the discussions.

2. Williams would initiate a telephone conference call the next day with presidents, executive secretaries, and the NEA director for South Carolina to discuss the memorandum.

3. The PEA Executive Committee would meet March 29, 1967, to discuss the memorandum. If adopted, the PEA House of Delegates would meet April 1.

According to Mr. Solomon, elected officers from the NEA and a staff representative from the NEA came to South Carolina to meet with certain PEA leaders to persuade them to accept the merger plan.

Inasmuch as the general policy of the NEA provided for notification of the executive secretary when high-ranking NEA officials are in a state, he was quite surprised when he learned from a PEA staff member of their presence.

Members of the PEA Executive Committee met, adopted the memorandum of agreement to the plan, and directed Mr. Solomon to call or write the county presidents to meet the next night. The NEA president, a member of NEA's Executive Committee from Southeast, and the NEA Southeast director were present for this meeting of county presidents. This was the first time that Mr. Solomon had seen either of the three. The county presidents accepted the memorandum of agreement and the explanations made by the three visitors.

The House of Delegates met, discussed the memorandum of agreement, and adopted it and the merger plan as one document on April 1, 1967. The NEA Executive Committee member from the Southeast was present for this meeting. Telegrams about the decision were sent to NEA officers, SCEA officers, and the NEA Southeast director by W. E. Solomon.

Proposed Plan for Unification of SCEA and PEA

(Rejected by the House of Delegates, March 4, 1967. Adopted with Memorandum of Agreement (dated March 22, 1967) on April 1, 1967.)

I. *Name:* The name of the new association shall be THE SOUTH CAROLINA EDUCATION ASSOCIATION. A new charter shall be drafted and recorded with the Secretary of the State.

II. *Officers (1 year term, 1967–68):* Dr. J. G. McCracken, President; Mrs. Ellen C. Watson, Vice-President; and Dr. Carlos W. Gibbons, Executive-Secretary.

III. *Board of Directors:* The Board of Directors of the new association shall be set up on an interim basis for a one (1) year period. The Executive Committee of each association will continue to serve during the interim period. (PEA has 18 members and SCEA has 21 members.) During the one year interval the full Board of Directors shall meet at least three (3) times. An interim executive committee, composed of the president and three members of each association, appointed from the Board of Directors, will meet more frequently to facilitate the work of the association. No members will be elected to either Board of Directors during 1967 and those whose terms expire will serve during the one year interim period.

At the end of the one year period, directors shall be elected by a majority vote of the membership. The number on the Board of Directors after the one year passed, shall be one from each of the judicial districts, or as determined in equalizing the teaching population in the districts, with the presidents of the following departments: Department of Classroom Teachers, Department of School Administrators, Department of Higher Education, Department of Education. In addition to those listed above the following shall serve on the Board: President, President-elect, Immediate Past President, Executive Secretary, NEA Director. (Should South Caroina qualify for two NEA Directors, they shall rotate as members of the Board.)

One of the three plans shall be used as a basis for the district organization of the new associations, or such re-districting as may be required to give all district directors proportionate representation. All directors shall be elected in March, 1968 in accordance with SCEA constitution, with staggered terms being ascertained.

IV. *Commissions and Committees:* Membership on state commissions and committees shall be based on the ratio of the membership of the two associations for one year transition period. There shall be at least three members from PEA on each commission and at least two members from PEA on each committee. The Professional Rights and Responsibilities Commission shall have equal representation during the interim period, and the Defense–Welfare Fund shall be maintained for the defense of teacher rights, however, any additional contribution to the fund will be recommended by the Professional Rights and Responsibilities Commission to the Board of Directors. The Professional Rights and Responsibilities Commission shall study the procedures of SCEA and PEA for grievance cases and recommend any change deemed desirable. The commissions shall consist of Professional Rights and Responsibilities (with emphasis upon "Defense of Teacher Rights"), Legislative, Teacher Education and Professional Standards, Public Relations, Welfare, Publications and Policy Planning. The PR&R Commission shall consist of nine members, four from PEA, four from SCEA, President of PEA serving as chairman. There shall be a two-thirds vote of the Board of Directors regarding recommendations made from the PR&R Commission. All other commissions shall have at least three members from PEA serving on each Commission.

The Standing Committees shall consist of Constitution and Bylaws, Resolutions, Finance, Necrology, Elections. The constitution and bylaws committee shall consist of nine members, four from PEA, four from SCEA, with the President of SCEA serving as chairman. All other committees shall have at least two members from PEA serving on each committee.

At the end of the one year period, membership on commissions and committees shall be filled without regard to race. Appointments to committees and commissions shall be made by the president. Chairmanships of commissions or committees shall be made by the president by a vote of the membership of such committee or commission.

V. *Delegate Assembly:* The general policies of the new association shall be determined by the Delegate Assembly. The membership in the Delegate Assembly shall be based on a formula related to the state association membership in the counties. (See Plans I, II, III for clarification.)

VI. *Staff:* The Executive Secretary of the SCEA shall be the Executive Secretary of the new association. The Executive Secretary of the Palmetto Education Association shall serve as Association Executive Secretary for Special Services.

The total staff of the South Carolina Education Association and the Palmetto Education Association shall serve in the new association during the interim period. No staff member will be reduced in salary during the interim period and all salaries are set annually by the Board of Directors.

The Executive Secretary shall recommend to the Board of Directors all staff positions after the one year interim period. Recommendations shall be made on basis of competence and qualifications and without regard to race. Clerical and secretarial appointments shall be made by the Executive Secretary in consultation with staff directors. Professional staff employed during the interim period shall not be discharged because of race, but are subject to existing policies relating to personnel.

VII. *Constitution:* After the plan is approved by the governing bodies, a joint committee of nine members shall be appointed to develop a constitution to govern the new association, four members from PEA, four members from SCEA and president of SCEA to serve as chairman.

Constitutional modifications during interim period: The PEA and SCEA Constitutions are to be amended or waivered by the House of Delegates and Council of Delegates to permit the following: SCEA not to elect a president-elect in 1967; PEA president to serve as vice-president of new organization for 1967-68; statewide candidate for president and president-elect in 1968, with office of vice-president being dissolved; and all members of the Board of Directors to be elected in 1968 with staggered terms being ascertained.

VIII. *Welfare Programs:* All members of the new association shall immediately become eligible for all the benefits of the SCEA and PEA, including life insurance, automobile insurance, home insurance, teacher annuity, mutual funds, life stock, hospitalization and accident insurance, etc.

IX. *Recommendations for Local Associations:* Any local affiliated with the NEA which has racial restrictions in the membership provisions should take steps to remove them as soon as possible. The locals which have no restrictions or which have removed such restrictions should set up joint committees to work toward merger of the local associations as soon as it is possible to do so.

Eventual merger of county associations is expected; however, this may take more than one year in some counties. State membership will not effect existing local option provisions. If complete merger of the state associations is accomplished by 1968, county associations should work toward complete merger by April, 1969.

X. *Dues:* The dues for the new association shall be $20 until changed by established procedures. Department dues shall be determined by a majority vote of the members of the department, or as specified in the existing departmental constitution. All members of the new association shall be required to be members of the state association before being permitted to actively participate in the work of the departments.

XI. *Property:* All property of the two associations shall become the property of the new association. This includes all assets and liabilities after concurrence by both associations and after legal counsel has advised positions relative to tangible ownerships, etc. Neither the PEA nor SCEA is to liquidate any assets after December 1, 1966 unless such liquidation is made known to the joint merger committee and the board of directors of both organizations. The PEA Defense–Welfare Fund will remain intact for the purposes stated above. There shall be a two-thirds vote of the Board of Directors regarding disposition of property.

XII. *Headquarters:* The headquarters of the new association shall be the new SCEA building. The headquarters of the Palmetto Education Association will be sold, rented, or liquidated as the Board of Directors deem best and instructs.

XHI. *Procedure:* If this plan is approved by the PEA–SCEA Merger Committee it shall be presented to the Executive Board of each association jointly. Each Executive Board shall act on the proposal. Then the plan shall be presented to the House of Delegates and the Council of Delegates respectively at the March 1967 convention and, if approved, go into effect on April 1, 1967 at the state level. (This is the interim plan.)

XIV. *Effective Date of Complete Merger:* The new association shall be officially declared as one as of April 1, 1968.

XV. *Position of Association after April 1, 1968:* each member shall have one vote; every member shall have the right to hold office; every member shall have all the rights and privileges of membership without regard to race; and no individual or group shall be given any special consideration because of race.[6]

Memorandum of Agreement

TO: Mr. Walker Solomon, Executive Secretary, PEA
     Mrs. Ellen Watson, President, PEA
     Dr. Carlos Gibbons, Executive Secretary, SCEA
     Mrs. Alice Mangum, President, SCEA
     Miss Gladys Robinson, NEA Director for South Carolina
FROM: James H. Williams, Southeastern Representative, NEA

The following points were agreed upon as clarification of the merger proposal between the Palmetto Education Association and the South Carolina

Education Association in a conference in Atlanta, Georgia, on Tuesday, March 21, 1967, and confirmed in a telephone conference call held at 10:00 A.M. on Wednesday, March 22, 1967.

1. It is understood that the constitution of the new association would be ratified by the policy-making bodies of the two associations (House of Delegates and Council of Delegates). In the event an acceptable proposed constitution is not agreed upon during the one-year interim period, it is understood that the interim period would automatically be extended beyond a year.

2. It is understood that all staff of the Palmetto Education Association will be employed with no reduction in salary with continuous employment on the same basis as other regular employees of the new association.

3. It is understood that Mr. Walker Solomon would be employed by the new association as Associate Executive Secretary for Special Services. The recommended salary range for this position would be the $13,000–$15,000 bracket. This position would have status above the position of a Division Director. The responsibilities would include teacher welfare, library, research, PR&R, legislation, and others. Dr. Carlos Gibbons expressed his desire that Mr. Walker Solomon remain with the SCEA because of the valuable contributions he could offer to the association and the continuity it would offer to the PEA membership.

It is understood that any obligation regarding personnel of the PEA made prior to the agreement of the plan would be honored by the new association.

4. It is understood that an attorney has been retained by the SCEA to handle cases referred by the PR&R Committee and Executive Board. It is further understood that any member has the right to appeal his case to national organizations for assistance after having exhausted the remedies provided by the new association.

5. It is understood that immediately upon merger that an integrated committee would be appointed to plan the leadership conference at Myrtle Beach, South Carolina, and that activities of the new association henceforth would be integrated.

6. It is understood that the above parties would accept and support these points of clarification to the merger proposal of the PEA and SCEA.

7. It is understood that a meeting will be called of the PEA Executive Committee on Wednesday, March 29, 1967, and a meeting of the House of Delegates on April 1, 1967, to consider the merger.

As important as a merger of the two associations was there was another achievement in 1966 that deserves special recognition. For 20 years, beginning with the administration of President Gallman, every president of the Palmetto Education Association urged the

135

state Department of Education to employ qualified Negroes to administer some of its programs. The first Negro employee was W. T. Gantt who was employed in the Speech and Hearing Correction Program. He was succeeded by Frank Washington.

The second person employed was Dr. Sylvia P. Swinton as assistant elementary school supervisor. Dr. Swinton was later succeeded by Miss Alfreda James. During 1966 five new appointments of Negroes were made by the state Department of Education. They were E. M. Wiley, assistant general supervisor, Division of Instruction; James D. Kibler, assistant supervisor of guidance, Title B; Dr. Gerard A. Anderson, assistant state coordinator, Adult Education; Miss Mary F. Griffin, evaluator of Library Projects, Title II; and James E. Jackson, assistant supervisor, Office Occupations.

CHAPTER VIII

The Executive Committee and the House of Delegates

The proper function of a government is to make it easy for the people to do good and difficult for them to do evil.

Sir William Blackstone

Between 1920 and 1936 the Executive Committee of the Palmetto State Teachers Association had control of the work of the Association. Article VIII of the Constitution stated that this committee "shall have general charge of the work of the Association, and shall have power to do all that may be necessary to fulfill the purpose of the Association."[1]

The first Executive Committee was listed in the March 1920 *Bulletin.* The chairman was G. W. Howard of Georgetown. The other members were Dr. R. S. Wilkinson of Orangeburg, Dr. R. W. Mance of Columbia, Dr. L. M. Dunton of Orangeburg, T. L. Duckett of Columbia, Miss Della Harvey of Beaufort, Miss Ellen Harvin of Manning, Mrs. C. G. Garrett of Columbia, A. W. Nicholson of Trenton, B. F. Hubert of Orangeburg, Dr. E. R. Roberts of Denmark, C. M. Young of Irmo, Mrs. Sarah Smalls Williams of Beaufort, and W. N. Arnold of Mullins.

In 1928 the composition of the Executive Committee was changed to conform with a provision of the new constitution which stated that this committee shall consist of "ten elected members with the President, Executive Secretary, Treasurer and Recording Secertary serving as ex-officio members."[2]

After complying with this provision the following persons were elected to the Executive Committee: Dr. R. S. Wilkinson, Dr. C. M.

Young, Dr. D. H. Sims, G. W. Howard, W. S. Montgomery, J. P. Burgess, E. A. Adams, Asa Thompson, J. L. Cain, and Mrs. Elise McLester. The ex-officio members were Dr. R. W. Mance, president of the Palmetto State Teachers Association; I. M. A. Myers, executive secretary; S. L. Finley, recording secretary; and Mrs. C. D. Saxon, treasurer.

The first minutes of this committee were published in the April 1923 *Bulletin*.[3] The executive secretary made a report of the Annual Meeting held in Spartanburg in March 1922. Among the items in his report were the increase in membership to 592 and the financial report which revealed a balance of $208.45 in the treasury. Mr. Myers also pointed out that the Association did not have enough funds to publish two issues of the *Bulletin* within a period of six months. In March 1922, the Executive Committee had requested the executive secretary to publish the proceedings within 60 days of the Annual Meeting which would have been no later than May 26. This was his reply to the questions the members raised in the December 30, 1922 meeting about his failure to comply with this request.

In March 1926 the Executive Committee made a recommendation to the Association changing the method of selecting a representative to the National Association of Teachers in Colored Schools (NATCS). Instead of being appointed by the president, the delegate was elected by the body.[4]

DISTRICT MEETINGS

Another recommendation of the Executive Committee which had a tremendous impact on the organization was made in March 1928 and laid the foundation for the district meetings:

> ... the Executive Committee of the State Colored Teachers Association would respectfully recommend that fall meetings be held in several sections of the State.

> It would be wise to hold one of these meetings in each Congressional District in October or early November. This would be a two-day conference, beginning on Friday morning and continuing through Saturday. All teachers and county superintendents from the counties in the Congressional District would be present to get inspiration and help for their work during the following months.

The executive committeeman from each district would be the general chairman of his district and the teachers of the council of delegates from this county would be his captains.[5]

The recommendation continues as follows:

At these fall meetings the teachers could get right down to brass tacks and go back to their schools with something that would mean something to the big mass of teachers who do not now feel any results. The counties could be organized and activities for the winter meetings planned for each county. The fall meeting would not interfere in the least with the annual spring meeting of the state Association except perhaps the spring convention would open on Thursday night instead of Thursday morning as it now does. The chairman feels that this would be a big forward step in the work of the Association and those to whom he has mentioned the idea have agreed most heartily.[6]

This particular recommendation was very significant and had a tremendous impact on the future growth and development of the organization. Not only did it lay the foundation for the district organization but it strengthened the county associations which provided more strength to the state organization. In addition, this recommendation placed great emphasis upon planning and involving more teachers in the affairs of the Association. This was not fully implemented until the fifties, but it was a giant step in the right direction.

Reference was made in Chapter II of a constitutional change in 1925 which provided for the election of members of the Executive Committee by congressional districts rather than the convention.

At the time this recommendation was submitted to the Association in 1928, the Executive Committee consisted of the following persons:

District 1. Joseph Berry, Charleston

District 2. W. D. Drake, Aiken

District 3. Miss Alice Webb, Anderson

District 4. W. A. Neal, Spartanburg

District 5. Mrs. Elise McLester, Camden

District 6. G. W. Howard, Georgetown

District 7. R. S. Wilkinson, Orangeburg

COMMITTEE EFFORTS TOWARD
EQUALITY IN EDUCATION

One of the most impressive reports made by any Executive Committee of the Palmetto State Teachers Association may be found in the March 1929 issue of the *Bulletin*. It begins with a reaffirmation of the faith of the Association in the principles of democracy and in public education. Then it proceeds to point out, with statistical documentation, the wide inequities in the educational expenditures for white and Negro children. One excerpt from the report stated:

> The Negro school houses are miserable beyond description. They are usually without comfort, equipment, proper lighting, or sanitation. Nearly all the Negroes of school age in the district are crowded in these miserable structures during the short term which the school runs. Most of the teachers are absolutely untrained and have been given certificates by the county board not because they have passed the examination but because it is necessary to have some kind of a Negro teacher.[7]

After pointing out these inequities the report makes a strong and urgent plea for equal educational opportunities.

This report also contained a criticism of the state department for failing to include information about Negro schools in its *Annual Handbook*: "Except for the list of accredited and non-accredited colleges no information of Negro educational programs appears in this departmental publication from year to year."[8]

In 1930 there were some changes in the Executive Committee. J. S. Shanklin replaced W. D. Drake in the Second District, Mrs. L. L. Sewell replaced W. A. Neal in the Fourth District, E. E. Riley replaced Mrs. Elise McLester in the Fifth District, and J. L. Cain replaced G. W. Howard in the Seventh District. This committee, under the chairmanship of Robert S. Wilkinson and during the presidency of C. A. Johnson, prepared a statement entitled *In Behalf of The State's Negro Children* and submitted it to the state legislature in an attempt to prevent further reductions in teachers' salaries. The economic situation during the early thirties brought about some proposals to reduce teachers' salaries, and the officials of the Palmetto State Teachers Association were desperately attempting to prevent any action from being taken on this matter by the members of the legislature. Some excerpts from the statement follow:

The officers of the Palmetto State Teachers Association, speaking for the Association's membership and in the name of the Negro teaching profession of South Carolina, reaffirm the Association's belief in the importance of education in community life and progress. We regret current proposals to retard needlessly the effectiveness of the schools by drastic reductions in the salary schedule for teachers. We regret these proposals because they involve a grave injustice to the schools and the teaching profession, because they would rob the children of the State of their just educational privileges.[9]

The future of South Carolina lies in the school house, for there is where citizens are made. Schoolhouses without well-prepared teachers become mere meeting houses. Members of the Palmetto State Teachers Association are deeply concerned about the present unhappy economic situation in general and particularly as it affects our state. We are interested and move to cooperate, as citizens, with the various relief agencies in their efforts to better conditions. We are convinced, however, that to reduce, at this time, the salaries of the teachers of the State would be most unfortunate—especially as this reduction would affect Negro education. We therefore respectfully call upon the Legislators of our state to reaffirm the American faith in education and to disfavor any attempt to handicap our children by driving the best teachers out of the profession. The rising generation should not be forced to a sacrifice of childhood's opportunity. South Carolina is resourceful enough to give every child his birthright—a generous education under the direction of trained and competent teachers.[10]

This statement contained some deplorable statistics concerning the status of Negro education in South Carolina at that time from 1930 to 1935. For example, the average monthly salary for Negro women was $37.98 and for Negro men, $50.34. In 1930 the State expended only 10 percent of the total educational expenditures for Negro education when Negro children constituted almost 50 percent of the school population. The ratio was the same in 1918. This meant that there was no relative improvement in the state allotment to Negro schools in 12 years.

As urgent as this appeal was and as convincing as the statistics were, the legislature did not act favorably upon their request. Not only did teachers get a 10 percent reduction in salaries, during one year they were paid in script.

When conditions did not improve after the economic depression of 1929–33, the Executive Committee decided to prepare a letter to be sent to all newspapers and influential white citizens to inform them of the tremendous handicap Negro teachers, administrators, and children were facing. This letter was mailed February 1936; it was signed by the members of the Executive Committee and the officers of the Association. At that time membership of the Executive Committee had changed again. The members were as follows:

District 1. Miss M. A. Broadnax, Charleston

District 2. J. S. Shanklin, Sr., Burton

District 3. Mrs. Alice W. Anderson, Anderson

District 4. J. T. W. Mims, Clinton

District 5. E. E. Riley, Lancaster

District 6. J. L. Cain, Darlington

District 7. C. W. Madden, Columbia

At-large   H. H. Butler, Hartsville

At-large   C. A. Johnson, Columbia

The officers in 1936 who also signed this letter were C. V. Bing, president; J. A. Holman, vice-president; Mrs. M. Alice La Saine, treasurer; S. L. Finley, recording secretary; and John P. Burgess, executive secretary.

According to Mr. Burgess, "the responses to that letter were exceedingly gratifying." The opening paragraphs follow:

> Considerable progress in the education of the Negro in South Carolina has been made in recent years, but today we find conditions rather deplorable. Our only hope seems to be an enlightened public opinion marked by a spirit of tolerance, good will and helpfulness and a willingness on the part of the leading white people of South Carolina to cooperate with us in a spirit of frankness in working for the improvement of Negro education.
>
> The seeming indifference of the white people of the State, we think, is due in a large manner to the fact that they do not know the real situation in which the education of the Negro finds itself.
>
> In recent years, we have had to bear a disproportionate share of the burden due to necessary curtailment of expenditures.[11]

Following these opening statements the committee quoted some unbelievable statistical data to support its position. It was pointed out that the 1934 report of the state superintendent stated that 8,319 white teachers were employed to teach 257,870 white children, and only 4,634 Negro teachers were hired to teach 228,842 Negro children. The average cost per white pupil was $41.75 as compared with $8.03 per Negro pupil. Also mentioned was the disproportionate share of federal aid the Negro schools were receiving. Forty-eight percent of the school population was Negro and received only nine percent of the federal aid appropriation. Also included in the letter was information about the length of the school terms and bus transportation. In 1933–34, according to the records of the state Department of Education, 1,315 of the 2,259 schools for Negroes were in operation only four months of the year. In that same year the state spent $809,410 to transport white children as compared with $939 for Negro children.[12]

The letter ends with this paragraph:

> The Palmetto State Teachers Association, through its Executive Committee, is appealing to the civic, political, industrial, educational and religious leaders of the white people of South Carolina to assume the leadership in building in our State a wholesome public sentiment which will assure adequate support for the education of the Negroes in this State.[13]

Indicative of some of the responses to the letter are two editorials which were published in the March 1936 issue of the *Bulletin*. One, taken from the *Southern Christian Advocate,* stated:

> Enlightened self interest alone should dictate to us a more liberal attitude of the Negro in South Carolina. We owe them educational and religious consideration and cooperation, and we are not faithful to ourselves until we discharge this obligation.[14]

The other editorial first appeared in the *State* on Sunday, February 16, 1936, three days after the *Advocate* editorial, with this comment: "The *State* believes the corporate conscience of white South Carolina is reopening fast toward readiness for effective awakening regarding this undischarged obligation."[15]

As we look back at the tremendous obstacles which faced these officers as they struggled so valiantly to get so little, we acquire a new sense of appreciation for their efforts. Lacking any political clout and having little influence on the white power structure, they used the only other method they knew—appealing to the conscience and the enlightened self interest of those who controlled the purse strings of the state. One of the great evils of the segregated system was that Negroes had to struggle against great odds to get what was already theirs. It was almost another decade before any substantial improvements were made in equalizing educational opportunities, and that was in the form of legal actions in the courts provided by the National Association for the Advancement of Colored People. This will be discussed in more detail in Chapter XIII.

1935: HOUSE OF DELEGATES, NEW GOVERNING BODY

The rapid growth of the Palmetto State Teachers Association during the decade of the thirties brought about a significant change in the governance of the organization. From 1920 to 1936 the controlling body was the Executive Committee. In 1935 the constitution was revised and one of the major provisions was the creation of the House of Delegates, a more broadly based governing body. The governance was shifted from the seven districts to the 46 counties and private schools and colleges. The exact provisions for this new legislative body may be found in Chapter II.

The authority to transact the business of the Association at the Annual Meeting was vested in the House of Delegates who reported to the Association. The remaining duties of the Executive Committee were appointing the executive secretary who must be approved by the House of Delegates and selecting the time and place of the annual meetings.

The power of the House of Delegates was greatly increased by Article V, Section E, which required all nominations for officers of the Association brought to it before being brought to the floor of the convention. Two names for each position were presented to the convention from the House.

The number of standing committees were increased in the constitution of 1935. In addition to committees on Auditing, Resolutions, Necrology, Constitution, and Ways and Means provided by the first constitution, the new one made provisions for standing committees on the President's Address, Ethics, and Tellers of Elections.

In 1939, the constitution was amended to spell out more specifically the powers of the Executive Committee. Article V, Section 5, states:

> ... the Executive Committee, subject to the provisions of this constitution and the directions of the House of Delegates shall have general charge of the activities of the Association between annual meetings of the same, and shall have power to do all that may be necessary to fulfill the purposes of the Association as herein set forth. It shall devise and assist the president in the preparations of programs and in the arrangement of meetings of the Association and its departments. It shall control receipts and expenditures and make contracts. It shall determine salaries, per diems, committee expenses, clerical help and pay, and office expenses.[16]

Several members of the House of Delegates were still dissatisfied with a number of provisions of the Constitution adopted by the body on March 15, 1935, which is referred to earlier. Members of the Committee on Revision of the Constitution appointed by President Anderson made its report on March 8, 1939; after two lengthy sessions each article was read and adopted section by section. The House finally adopted the entire constitution on March 9, 1939 with the suggested revisions and amendments. The members of this committee were J. L. Cain, K. W. Green, I. M. A. Myers, N. C. Nix, and T. H. Pinckney. This constitution remained as adopted until 1957 when another revision was effected.

1941: INCORPORATION OF PSTA

In April 1941, the House of Delegates recommended that the Executive Committee be instructed to secure a charter for the Palmetto State Teachers Association. The Executive Committee acted upon this recommendation and the Association became legally incorporated under the laws of South Carolina on July 23, 1941.[17]

This was a great achievement for the developing organization. It needed the status, the stability, and the recognition that this action provided.

CONTINUING APPEALS FOR EQUALITY IN EDUCATION

At this same meeting of the House of Delegates in April 1941, the Executive Committee reported that it had "appeared before a committee appointed by the Governor by request of the legislature and made known the things that in the opinion of the Negro teachers in South Carolina need to be adjusted."[18] At this meeting with this special committee, the Executive Committee through President John P. Burgess presented a six-point request:

1. Teachers with similar training and performing the same class of work to be paid the same salary.

2. Equalization to begin with the 1941–42 school year.

3. Complete equalization in two years.

4. Operation of all schools not less than eight months.

5. At least one accredited high school in each county free of tuition to all children in the county.

6. Transportation where needed.[19]

It was at this period in the history of the Palmetto State Teachers Association that some of the members of the organization became impatient with the state legislature for its failure to take action on the appeals of the Executive Committee. This dissatisfaction was expressed in the House of Delegates and suggestions for a different procedure to obtain equalization of salaries and other educational reforms were expressed. On April 3, 1941 the president of the Columbia chapter of the National Association for the Advancement of Colored People, the Reverend E. A. Adams, was presented to the House of Delegates to make some remarks, and he urged the members not to accept any compromise on salary equalization.[02]

The next day, April 4, the House passed a resolution earmarking 25 percent of the money received as membership fees to serve as a teacher defense fund.

It was becoming increasingly obvious to many teachers that the struggle for equal education opportunities and facilities would have to be settled in the courts. Appealing to the conscience and the enlightened self interest of those in control had failed.

A more detailed account of the action taken by the Executive Committee and the House of Delegates in the implementation of other procedures to secure educational equality may be found in Chapter XIII. The remainder of this chapter will deal with the decisions made and actions taken by both of these bodies to continue the forward movement of the Association.

On November 17, 1951, the House of Delegates took a giant step forward when it adopted the following policies recommended by the Program and Policies Committee, chaired by H. L. Barksdale:

1. County presidents submit from 3 to 5 names in his County Association for appointment to PSTA standing committees.

2. Officers and appointees to standing committees should pay PSTA membership for fiscal year upon acceptance of position.

3. There should be a planning conference for the Association each year in September.

4. That the officers of the Association should meet three (3) times per year and as often thereafter as emergencies may dictate.

5. That the district chairmen attend at least one meeting per year of each county in his district.

6. That district chairmen hold one or more meetings with their county presidents.

7. That district chairmen encourage organization of the PSTA in the following areas: Department of Secondary and Elementary Principals, of Classroom Teachers and of FTA Chapters.

8. That a building plan of appointment and election be the policy of the Association.

9. That there should be a closer working together of the PSTA and the State Congress of PTA.

10. That a public relations program be designed which will solicit and promote public interest in the cause of education.[21]

Another forward step was taken on March 27, 1952 when the House added six more policy statements to the ten already adopted:

1. That the harmonious and full support of the NAACP be maintained and continued.

2. That outstanding projects in county meetings be sent to the Executive Secretary and distributed to the counties through publication in the *Journal*.

3. That the PSTA continue to press for personnel in the State Department of Education.

4. That registration and voting become a part.of the regular business of each county organization.

5. That the amount of reserve for depreciation as recommended by the auditing firm of Mohrmann and Wohltmann be set aside each year.

6. That 20 percent of membership fees be earmarked and set aside for the building fund.[22]

The fifth policy statement had implications for the Finance Committee and suggested the need for budgetary policies for the Association. On March 26, 1953 John F. Potts, chairman of the Finance Committee, presented to the House of Delegates a list of budgetary policy statements which were adopted unanimously.[23]

STANDING COMMITTEES

The first Constitution adopted by the Association in 1922 designated four standing committees—Finance, Resolutions, Necrology, and Constitution. As the years passed, the number of standing committees increased. In the 1957 revised Constitution this provision was made for standing committees: "The Association shall have as many standing committees as may be deemed necessary to carry on the work of the Association."[24] This was a wise and necessary provision because the House of Delegates and the Executive Committee needed wide latitude in steadily building a strong Association. The organization grew so rapidly that by 1952 it had created a total of 16 standing committees. At that time there were committees on Constitution, Building, Entertainment, Ethics, Finance, Legislation, Membership, Necrology, Policies, Program Research, Resolutions, Retirement, and Tenure. There were also standing committees for Tax Education and School Finance and Teacher Education and Professional Standards (TEPS). However, by 1966, there were some changes in the committees although the total number remained the same. The PEA standing committees and chairpersons in 1966–67 were Civic Education, C. C. Cole; Constitution, Mrs. Virginia J. Marion; Credit Union, E. J. Bonaparte; Educational Finance, Dr. E. A. Finney, Sr.; Ethics, Mrs. A'la Perle Hickman; Finance, Allen L. Cole; Legislative, Dr. Allen Williams; Membership, Wilmot J. Fraser; Policies, Mrs. D. Maude Shelle; Public Relations, Mrs. Bernie C. Duckett; Research, Dr. I. C. Bracey; Resolutions, Rev. Ruben Dicks; Retirement, W. L. Hamilton. The Commissions were Professional Rights and Responsibilities, Larrie J. Foster; Teacher Education and Professional Standards, B. M. Wakefield; and the TEPS Associate Members.

CHANGES IN THE EXECUTIVE COMMITTEE

There were very few changes in the constitution affecting the House of Delegates, but the Executive Committee was changed to include presidents of the Department of Classroom Teachers, the Department of Secondary Principals, the Department of Elementary Principals, the Department of County Presidents, one person representing the colleges and private schools, and a liaison officer. These

The Executive Committee, 1954.

The Executive Committee, 1960-61.

were added to those persons who qualified under the previous provision, namely, the president, vice-president, treasurer, two members-at-large, six elected from the Districts, and the past president. The total number on the Executive Committee was increased to 18.

Reference has already been made to the following actions taken by the Executive Committee and the House of Delegates:

1. The adoption of a Statement of Principles to which the Association adhered

2. The approval of a list of goals the Association was striving to attain

3. The adoption of a Code of Ethics

4. The establishment of a Teacher Welfare–Defense Fund

5. The approval of the unification plan to merge the PEA with the SCEA.

FINANCIAL AFFAIRS

Since all financial transactions of the Association were in the final analysis the responsibility of the Executive Committee and the House of Delegates, some information about the handling of fiscal affairs should be provided at this point. All increases in dues had to be approved by the House of Delegates. Budgets were adopted and the executive secretary made an annual financial report supported by an auditor's report to the House.

Income and expenditures increased from 1920 to 1964. In 1919–20, the income was $508 compared with $99,029.46 in 1963–64 (this does not include dues collected for NEA and ATA). During those same years, the expenditures totaled $336.83 for 1919–20 and $92,051.96 in 1963–64. The most significant aspect of this financial arrangement is that the Association not only kept expenditures in line with income, but in some years it actually had some rather substantial balances. This was done in spite of earmarking funds for purchasing the first headquarters property, building the new administrative center, and maintaining a substantial Teacher Welfare–Defense Fund. For a period of more than 45 years, the PEA had record of good financial management.

The accompanying chart shows the financial growth of the Association. At the time of merger, the Association's real property and other assets debt free were as follows:

1. Administration Center, $100,000

2. Furniture and equipment, $25,000

3. Buick station wagon, $5,000

4. Held in Victory Savings Bank:
   Operational Fund, $56,000
   Defense Welfare Fund, $50,000
   Building Maintenance Fund, $10,000

5. To be collected from exhibitors (104) and advertisers, $9,000
   Membership processing, NEA, $1,200

FINANCIAL GROWTH OF THE PEA
1920-1966

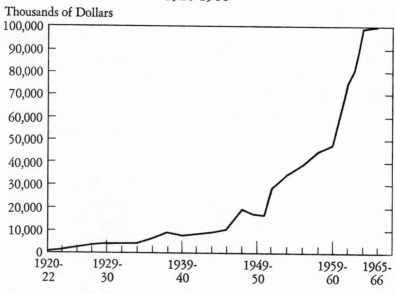

CHART 3.

152

CHAPTER IX

County Associations and District Meetings

If a man empties his purse into his head, no man can take it away from him. An investment in knowledge always pays the best interest.

Benjamin Franklin

County teachers' associations were organized before the Palmetto State Teachers Association came into existence. However, they were small autonomous groups with no structured connection with any state organization. In Chapter I it was pointed out that "only a few counties attended the annual meetings (state), yet invitations were sent yearly either to all organized county associations or to influential educators in counties where there were no county associations."[1] The county associations which ante-dated the Palmetto State Teachers Association emerged from the county institutes that were conducted by Edward Wallace, J. L. Cain, and other education leaders, between 1895 and 1900.

The founders of the state organization very wisely made provisions in the first constitution to involve those counties already in existence and to motivate the organizing of county associations in those counties where none existed. Among the most important provisions were the following:

1. An advisory council consisting of the presidents of the county associations was established.

2. A refund of 25 cents out of every dollar of membership dues was returned to the counties for their operational expenses.

These provisions were designed to make the county associations an integral part of the new state organization. An additional illustration of the importance of the county associations was the publication of the name of each member by county in the *Teacher's Directory* which helped stimulate the acquiring of new members.

John P. Burgess, the executive secretary from 1928 to 1940, made this observation about the county organizations: "Through its refund to the Counties the Association has helped to build up strong county organizations in which its members meet monthly to study and discuss their problems."[2]

He also mentioned some other ways the Association aided the counties:

> Last summer the state association helped to pay the salaries of eigheen instructors in the summer schools, thus making it possible for eleven summer schools of the state to meet their financial obligations better. It has consistently supported the National Association of Teachers in Colored Schools by paying its affiliation dues and by sending strong representatives to its convention to bring back to us inspiration and information gained through contact with outstanding educators and administrators from every section of the nation where separate schools are maintained for our group.[3]

The county associations became even stronger in January 1951 when all of the county presidents were called together by President Parler to hear the recommendations he was submitting to strengthen the Association. This meeting was called during one of the critical periods of the Association. It had just experienced some unfavorable publicity associated with the certification examination and was without the services of an executive secretary for six months. Memberships were decreasing, and interest in the Association was waning. Something needed to be done to get the Association moving forward again.

1951: DEPARTMENT OF COUNTY PRESIDENTS ORGANIZED

As soon as Mr. Solomon, the new executive secretary, took office on December 1, 1950 Mr. Parler asked him to call a meeting as soon as possible of all county presidents. Mr. Solomon immediately sent out notices for a January 6 meeting. Thirty-seven of the forty-six county presidents attended this meeting in Allen University's library and voiced approval of all of the recommendations proposed by Mr. Parler (see Chapter V). As further willingness of their desire to support the Association during this unsettled period, the county presidents decided to organize themselves into a permanent department of the Palmetto State Teachers Association. The officers are listed in Chapter V. This was a very significant step for the county presidents and paved the way for the counties to gather even more strength in the future.

One of the first steps the newly organized department took was writing and adopting a constitution related to the constitution of the Palmetto Education Association. The purposes of the organization were stated as follows:

1. To provide unification for the state programs

2. To promote an appreciation for ethical practices in the profession

3. To encourage uniformity in county organizations.[4]

The key words in these statements of purposes are "unification," "uniformity," and "ethical practices." The county presidents were creating a new instrument designed to unite the state organization, provide uniform procedures for action, and make all members more aware of the need to be ethical in relationships with others.

The membership was limited to all county presidents and the president and executive secretary of the Palmetto Education Association. Meetings were held twice annually, and an annual fee of $2 was paid by each county to pay for operational expenses.

Each county association was requested by the executive secretary to submit annually a form providing such information as names, addresses, and telephone numbers of officers and committee chairmen; schedule of year's meeting dates; goals for the coming year; local problems to be overcome; and special projects.

In addition to submitting this basic information form, a more detailed report form prepared by the executive secretary was requested from each county president. In reality it was more than a report form; it was also a rating sheet because points were given for the specific accomplishments listed and actions taken.

The county associations also received some very helpful services from the state organization. Job descriptions for the county president, vice-president, secretary, and treasurer were prepared and sent to each county association. Organizational aids were made available to help each county organize its department in a form consistent with all other counties and the state organization. For example, the state organization had 16 standing committees, and each county was expected to set up 16 parallel committees in order for the Palmetto Education Association to operate in a united and uniform way. The relationship of the county organization to the district organization was clarified. Specialists and consultants were provided when needed.

Publications, including the *Journal,* newsletters, research information, minutes and reports of departments, and actions by the South Carolina legislature were sent regularly to each county. Investigations were made of any unfair treatment of members. Planning conferences and workshops were held to train officers to more efficiently and effectively carry out their duties. This "planning togetherness" also brought about more unity.

County Presidents

LEADERSHIP CONFERENCES

After the organizational meeting on January 6, 1951, the county president's association met in the fall and spring of each year. These meetings demonstrated the need for the Association to schedule two annual conferences. The first usually met in August and was called a Leadership Conference. To this three-day meeting "the county associations sent four persons to participate in discussions, present problems, and hear suggested projects for their associations."[5] One of the special purposes of this conference was to give each county representative an opportunity to learn the purpose and functions of the Palmetto Education Association committees.

PLANNING CONFERENCES

The second conference usually met in September and was referred to as a Planning Conference. Invited to this affair to plan the program of the Association were the county presidents and secretaries, members of standing committees, representatives from the Department of Classroom Teachers, and the persons in charge of the Unified Enrollment Plan in each county. This plan was a joint project of PEA and NEA and emphasized the payment of county, state, ATA, and NEA dues at one time.

These two conferences were tremendous assets to the Association and account in a large measure for its steady growth and organizational strength.

Mr. Solomon also arranged for district planning meetings to review programs, discuss problems, and plan for district meetings. Officers of county associations, district committee chairpersons, presidents of departments, and members of the House of Delegates were invited to these district planning meetings.

DISTRICT MEETINGS

In March 1925 the Constitution Committee revised the constitution to give the congressional districts rather than the total membership the authority to elect the members of the Executive Committee. This reduced the ten elective members to seven and established the congressional district as a significant part of the organizational structure of the state association. In Chapter VIII reference is made to a recommendation of the Executive Committee in March 1928 that laid the foundation for the district meetings. It was suggested that each congressional district hold one of its meetings during October or November. The executive committee member from each district had the responsibility for presiding over the meeting and planning the program.

It was anticipated that this fall meeting would not change the annual spring meeting. Rather, it would strengthen the organization by bringing professional improvement to the district, county, and classroom level. This arrangement would also improve communications among these segments of the Association. This recommendation was accepted and the dates of these fall district meetings were scheduled by the Executive Committee. As the Palmetto State Teachers Association grew in size, the district meetings assumed more significance. The president and the executive secretary could contact the teachers in all of the counties in one year by attending these district meetings. This could not be accomplished on the county level.

Whenever a problem arose which needed the full participation and consideration of the entire membership, it was referred to a special committee composed of at least one member from each congressional district. This was especially true when the Association was struggling with the equalization of salaries issue. A special committee was elected from the six districts in 1945 to work with the NAACP in planning the legal strategies for salary equalization and other educational inequities.

In 1950, when the Association qualified for 21 delegates to the ATA, each district was requested to elect three delegates to represent it at the Annual Convention. Prior to this time the delegates were elected by the House of Delegates.

This same procedure was used after 1958 to enable each district to elect at least one delegate to the NEA convention. Before the Association had enough members in the NEA to qualify for seven delegates, they were elected by the House of Delegates. With the increase in NEA memberships which increased the number of delegates from the Palmetto Education Association, this authority was delegated to the districts.

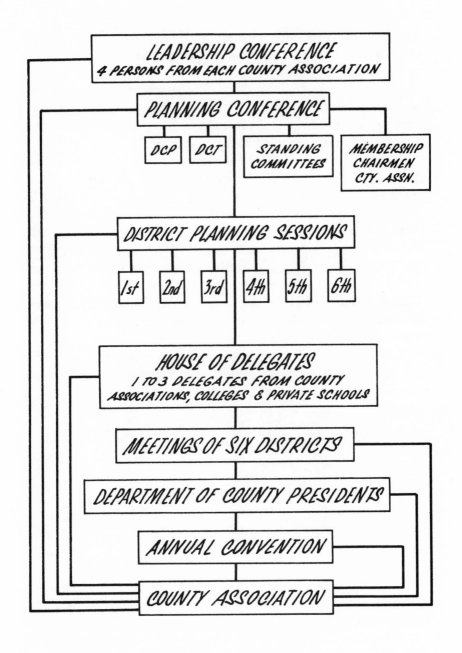

CHART 4. ORGANIZATION OF PEA, 1962

When the Association changed its organizational structure in 1959, it established 16 standing committees on the state level. To provide unity and uniformity, each district was requested to name parallel district committees. The state committee member served as chairperson of the district committee. This arrangement made it possible for all districts to act in concert. Likewise, the district member of this committee served as chairperson of the county committee in that district. This provided complete coordination of action from the county through the district to the state organization. To bring about even more unity the duties of all standing committees were described in detail and mailed to each committee member.

All of these structural changes in the organization in the Association illustrate the important position of the district organization. The power of the district is further demonstrated by its authority to elect six members of the Executive Committee, the second most powerful decision-making body of the Association. These same elected members of the Executive Committee were also presidents of the district organizations.

This special attention which the Association gave to the counties and districts resulted in a stronger state organization which could operate in a unified way.

CHAPTER X

The Annual Conventions

Education is a debt due from the present to future generations.

George Peabody

The first annual convention of the Association for which we have any record was held in Columbia, South Carolina, at Benedict College and Allen University on March 18–20, 1920. Prior to that time the annual meetings were held each year at South Carolina State College in Orangeburg during the summer sessions. In 1918, Dr. Wilkinson, president of the college, suggested that the place of the annual meetings be changed so that the Association could operate independently rather than be conceived a part of the college's summer session. This suggestion was accepted by the officers of the organization, and thereafter the annual meetings were held in Columbia because of its central location.

CONVENTIONS DURING THE 1920's

It was estimated by the Reverend I. E. Lowery who wrote a report of the convention that there were approximately 500 persons in attendance at the 1920 session. The financial report revealed that $393 was collected from registration fees. These fees were paid by the counties and Allen University, Benedict College, State College, and Voorhees Industrial School.[1] At that time the new constitution which made a provision for the annual membership dues to be $1 had not been adopted. As a matter of fact, a recommendation was made during the 1921 convention which was held in Columbia at Benedict College and Allen University that fees not be collected:

> The State Teachers Association should not spend much time collecting fees. We need only sufficient funds each year to meet contingent expenses. If we coninue to stress the collection of finances

161

to the neglect of matters of more importance harm will be done and interest in the bigger propositions lessened. Also it may cause distrust and factions will be started.

Instead of making one dollar as annual fee for the requirement for membership in the State Teacher's Association, all teachers qualified by the State Board of Examiners shall be members of the Association.[2]

To collect sufficient funds to meet "contingent expenses it was recommended that a committee be appointed to request pledges from different schools."[3] It was soon discovered that this was not a very dependable financial arrangement, and the provision for annual membership dues of $1 was adopted by the Association.

The 1922 convention was held in Spartanburg. The general sessions were held in the auditorium of the Court House, the Silver Hill Methodist Church, and the Mt. Moriah Baptist Church. The group meetings were conducted in the Carey Street Graded School. Special arrangements were made for teachers to visit Cedar Springs School for Deaf and Blind.

The main address was delivered by Dr. James H. Dillard, president of the Slater and Jeanes Funds. His subject was "What Has the Negro Race Contributed to Civilization." Other speakers were officials from the state Department of Education and the president of the Association.

The next four conventions, beginning with 1923, were returned to Columbia. They followed the same format of the preceding ones except that beginning with the 1926 Convention, the opening session was held Wednesday evening at 8 p.m. rather than 10:30 Thursday morning. No convention themes were used until the 1926 session selected "More Days in School and Better Days Work" as its theme. There was one other distinguishing feature about the 1926 convention. It was the first time that the Palmetto State Teachers Association had any contact with the National Education Association. Miss Mary McSkimmon, president of the National Education Association and principal of Pierce Elementary School in Brookline, Massachusetts, delivered the main address to the convention.

The 1927 convention was held at the Phyllis Wheatly Center in Greenville. Some of the meetings were held in the Springfield Baptist Church. An invitation was extended to the teachers by Mr. Hollis, superintendent of the Parker School District, to visit the schools in this district which was located just outside the city limits of Greenville. Since the schools in the Parker district had received wide recognition for their good instructional practices, a large number of visiting teachers accepted the invitation.

A special feature of the 1928 convention held in Columbia was a cotton dress demonstration stressing the importance of cotton and its uses. This program was arranged and supervised by Miss Lillian Hoffman, state supervisor of home economics, and Miss Marian Gardner, home economics supervisor at South Carolina State College. It consisted of a pageant depicting the "Beginnings of Cotton," a state style show for high school and college girls, and a "Cotton Products March" by students from Waverly Elementary School. There was also a cotton dress contest for teachers. Young ladies from forty high schools and two colleges participated in the style show. First, second, and third prizes were awarded to Wilkinson High in Orangeburg, Avery Institute in Charleston, and Robert Smalls High in Beaufort.

S. L. Finley, the recording secretary for the convention, wrote the following commentary of the demonstration. "The program was, possibly, the most interesting one yet carried out at any association meeting. It dealt with the practical things of our everyday life—the making and wearing of things from cotton."[4]

The general sessions programs during the 1929 convention were probably the most inspirational of all during the decade of the twenties. Two eloquent, dynamic, and prominent speakers delivered the main addresses on Thursday and Friday nights. Dr. Mordecai Johnson, eminent president of Howard University, spoke to the Thursday night general session, and Dr. Channing H. Tobias, National YMCA secretary, was the speaker Friday night.

THEMES FOR CONVENTIONS IN THE 1930's

The theme of the 1935 convention was "Training for Character and Citizenship." This is the earliest reference to a theme to be found in the records, and this appears to be the first time that the departments as well as the speakers for the general sessions were requested to plan their programs and presentations around the theme. The keynote speakers for the evening sessions were Dr. Ambrose Caliver, senior specialist in the education of Negroes, Office of Education, and C. C. Spaulding, president of the North Carolina Mutual Life Insurance Company.

The 1936 convention theme was "Training for Life's Responsibilities." This theme permeated the entire convention from the primary group to the general sessions. One of the special features of this convention was the recognition of teachers who had taught 50 years or more. They were Henry Pearson, dean of Claflin College; A. W. Nicholson, Trenton; T. H. Sanders, Laurens; Thomas Gregory, Columbia; W. T. White, Richburg; Mrs. M. H. White, Spartanburg; Mrs. Emma Maddox, Ware Shoals; Mrs. Lula E. Johnson, Orangeburg; Mrs. Mary Jones, Chester; S. A. Williams, Marion; Sarah J. Mills; and Mrs. Alice J. Long, Newberry.[5]

The theme of the 1937 convention was "Preparation for Jobs" which elicited this comment from Dr. Gordon B. Hancock:

> A most inspiring bit of information comes from South Carolina. In many ways it is of great significance to Negroes everywhere. The Palmetto State Teachers Association composed of more than two thousand Negro teachers has arranged the program for its annual convention in March. The theme of the meeting is "Preparation for Jobs." If there has been any greater stroke of common sense manifested among Negroes within the last twenty-five years this writer does not recall it. Negro South Carolina is rising nobly to meet a trying challenge.[6]

This statement appeared in the *Norfolk Journal and Guide* on February 20, 1937. At that time Dr. Hancock was a regular columnist for this newspaper. His articles were entitled "Between the Lines."

The guest speaker for the 1937 convention was Dr. Benjamin E. Mays who at that time was dean of the School of Religion at Howard University.

After the use of convention themes for three years brought such wide acceptance and more unity and cohesiveness among the departments, they became a permanent part of the program planning. For the next three years the following themes were used: "Improvement of Home Life Through Education" in 1938, "The Teacher's Opportunity for Vocational Guidance" in 1939, and "Training for Economic Security" in 1940.

The guest speakers for these three years were Rufus J. Clement, president of Atlanta University; James E. Shepherd, president of

North Carolina State College for Negroes; and H. Council Trenholm, president of Alabama State Teachers College.

CONVENTIONS IN THE 1940's

The themes selected for the annual conventions during the decade of the forties by the program committees reflect the signs of the times and issues which confronted the Association. Four of the themes—"The School and National Defense" in 1941, "The Role of the School in a Nation at War" in 1943, "Education for Post War Peace" in 1944 and "Education for Peace and and Economic Security" in 1946—indicate how seriously World War II affected the Palmetto State Teachers Association. All of the keynote speakers prepared their addresses around these themes, and the chairpersons of the departments planned their programs in concert with the themes.

Because a disproportionate number of Negro youth was failing the physical examination for the armed forces, the Association selected "Health Education, A National Necessity" as a theme in 1942. Judge William Hastle, who at that time was civilian aide to the Secretary of War, was the featured speaker.

In 1943 there was no convention. There was instead a one-day meeting of the House of Delegates on April 9. This is described in more detail in Chapter III.

The other disturbing issues resulting from the impending court suits to equalize salaries and other educational inequities are reflected in the themes "Education for Democratic Living" in 1945 and "Education for the Improvement of Human Relations" in 1947.

Dr. M. F. Ashley Montagu was the main speaker in 1947. His book *Man's Most Dangerous Myth: The Fallacy of Race* is a monumental work in the area of human relations.

The 1948 theme was "Equal Opportunities for All Americans." The main speakers were Attorney Thurgood Marshall and Dr. Ambrose Caliver, senior specialist in the education of Negroes, Office of Education. Dr. W. H. Gray, Jr., president of Florida A & M College, spoke on the subject "What a Southern State is Doing Toward Providing Equal Opportunities for All of Its Citizens."

In 1949, the theme was "Education for the Improvement of Community Life." Dr. Channing Tobias, a member of President Truman's Committee on Civil Rights, delivered the keynote address.

165

CONVENTIONS IN THE 1950's

During the decade of the fifties there were only five convention themes used by the program planners. With one exception there is no explanation of this omission of the other five. Whatever the reason was for discontinuing the use of a convention theme in 1954, 1955, 1956, and 1959, the growth of the Association was not impaired. Quite to the contrary, the Palmetto Education Association experienced a period of unprecedented growth during the fifties and substantially strengthened its organizational structure. This was a period of "organizing for action" and it may have been precisely for this reason that themes were not used. Internal strengthening took precedence over external observances of a special theme. However, the themes of the annual conventions for 1950, 1952, 1953, 1957, and 1958 had some unifying influence upon the Association in that county associations' programs were related to themes of the state conventions.

The convention theme for 1950 was "Education for Complete Living." The featured speakers for this occasion were Dr. Ira De A. Reid, head of the Social Science Department of Haverford College, and Dr. Rufus Clement, president of Atlanta University. The Program Committee decided to offer the county associations a special theme for each month based upon the convention theme. In this way, the programs of the county associations became more closely identified with the convention program.

In 1951, Mr. E. M. Wiley was chairman of the convention program. The committee selected the following theme for the convention, "Government For and By the People." The two main speakers, Dr. J. J. Seabrook, president of Claflin College, and Dr. Mordecai W. Johnson, president of Howard University, delivered very stimulating addresses.

The convention theme for 1952 was "Creating Public Interest in Education." The main address was delivered by Dr. Horace Mann Bond, president of Lincoln University. One of the highlights of this convention was the adoption of a code of ethics.

In 1953 the theme was "Citizenship Education for a Period in Transition." The featured speakers at this convention were Dr. Lyle W. Ashby, assistant secretary of the NEA, Dr. Walter Daniel, Department of Higher Education, Office of Education; and Dr. Frank

Chase, dean of the School of Education, University of Chicago. At this convention a citation was given to Mrs. Eloise Key Pendarvis for becoming the five hundred thousandth teacher to be enrolled in the NEA. The Palmetto Education Association got nationwide publicity for this event.

At the thirty-sixth annual convention in 1954, the Reverend Archibald J. Carey, U.S. delegate to the United Nations, addressed the members of the Palmetto Education Association on April 1. He spoke out against segregation and discrimination and stated that the aims of the United Nations were world peace and the dignity of the individual.

On the following night, Friday, April 2, the Right Reverend Frank Madison Reid, presiding bishop of the Eighth Episcopal District, AME Church, addressed the teachers on the subject "Education Free From Fear." He told the teachers that the prevailing fears in education today made free inquiry impossible. To get the full import of this statement, one must recall that it was made six weeks before the historic May 17, 1954 Supreme Court decision and that the question of segregation in education had not been decided.

The thirty-seventh annual convention in 1955 was a "first" in many respects. For the first time in the history of the Association, a woman presided over the convention. It was also the first time a woman presided over the House of Delegates. For the first time both the president and the vice president were women—Dr. Madge Perry Harper and Mrs. Leila A. Bradby, respectively, held those offices. Also for the first time, all of the featured speakers of the convention were women. They were Dr. Mary McLeod Bethune, founder and president emeritus of Bethune-Cookman College; Dr. Margaret Just Butcher, a member of the Washington, D.C. School Board; and Dr. Deborah Partridge, professor of education, New York University. The Palmetto Education Association's "Statement of Principles" was also approved at this convention.

In 1957 the theme "An Educated People Moves Freedom Forward" was suggested by President Lelia A. Bradby and accepted by the Executive Committee. It was the same theme used by the National Education Association as it observed its one hundredth anniversary while the Palmetto Education Association was observing its one hundredth birthday. The keynote speakers were Dr. Ralph J. Bunche of the U.S. State Department and Dr. Howard K. Thurman, dean of

Marsh Chapel, Boston University. Two highlights of this convention were the observance of the National Education Association Centennial with a banquet and pageant and the organizing of the Department of Classroom Teachers. This was a history-making convention in that it was the first one held after the completion of the new Administration Center.

The convention theme for 1958 was "Human Relations: an Important Factor in Democratic Living." The speakers were Dr. Arthur D. Gray, president of Talladega College; Dr. S. E. Duncan, state supervisor of public instruction, Raleigh, North Carolina; and Dr. J. L. Wallace, president of West Virginia State College. All speakers emphasized the need for better human relations to deal with problems arising from the reversal of the segregated pattern of education.

As previously indicated, there was no theme for the forty-first annual convention in 1959. The principal speakers were Judge Mercer M. Mance, judge of the superior court, Marion County, Indiana; and Dr. Edward W. Brice, specialist in fundamental and literacy education, Office of Education, U.S. Department of Health, Education, and Welfare. Both of these speakers previously lived in South Carolina. Judge Mance's father was a former president of the Association, and Dr. Brice served as co-chairman of the Program Committee in 1950 when he was on the faculty at South Carolina State College.

CONVENTIONS IN THE 1960's

The annual conventions during the sixties were very impressive events. In 1960 the theme was "New Dimensions in Education." Dr. John W. Davis, president emeritus of West Virginia State College; Dr. Horace Mann Bond of Atlanta University; and Dr. Stephen J. Wright, president of Fisk University, were the convention speakers. The scholarly presentations of these distinguished educators were focused upon the concept that education today must be seen in different dimensions from those of yesterday.

The theme for the forty-third annual convention in 1961 was "Excellence in Education for a Decade of Decision in the 1960's." Dr. Samuel Gandy of Dillard University and Dr. Aaron Brown of the Phelps–Stokes Fund delivered the main addresses. Dr. Brown discussed the present status of education in South Carolina as compared with other states in the South and pointed out what needed to be done to meet the challenge of the sixties. Dr. Gandy stated that "excellence is the keynote of the spirit of the new frontier."[7] It was announced at this convention that the Palmetto Education Association had established a film library for the use of its members.

There was no new theme in 1962, but the convention provided some outstanding speakers for the occasion. The main addresses were delivered by Dr. Carl T. Rowan, U.S. State Department, Washington, D.C.; Dr. Don Davies, National Education Association; and Julius Thomas of the National Urban League. That year 17 of the 36 departments sponsored workshops, clinics, and student projects. For the first time "ninety-nine percent of the teachers employed in the public schools of South Carolina are members of their state association."[8]

In 1963 the theme of the forty-fifth annual convention was "Education for Responsibility in a Free Society." In addition to three major addresses by Hobart Taylor, Dr. Francis Chase of the University of Chicago, and Ewald Turner of the National Education Association which were enthusiastically received by the audiences, this convention was one of the best in terms of attendance. All membership records in Palmetto Education Association, American Teachers Association, and National Education Association were broken.[9]

"We Rededicate Ourselves" was the theme for the forty-sixth annual convention in 1964. The main addresses were delivered by Dr. Robert Weaver the Federal Housing Administration and Dr. Martin Jenkins, president of Morgan State College. Both messages were very inspirational and were well received. A "Code of Ethics for the Education Profession" was unanimously adopted by the House of Delegates, and the attendance at the 1964 convention was the highest the Association had ever experienced. At this convention there was also a symbolic burning of the mortgage on the new headquarters building. This was a great milestone in the history of the Association. The Administrative Center now belonged to the Palmetto Education Association.

In 1965 the theme was "Teacher Competence in an Automated Society." The main addresses were delivered by Dr. Luna I. Mishoe, president of Delaware State College and Whitney M. Young, executive director of the National Urban League. Both addresses provided so much valuable information that they were published in the May 1965 issue of the *Palmetto Education Association Journal.*

Because of the need for strong leadership to aid in merging the Palmetto Education Association and the South Carolina Education Association, the theme for 1966 was "Educational Leadership for a Critical Period." The principal addresses were delivered by two former South Carolinians, Dr. L. C. Dowdy, president of A and T University and Dr. Benjamin F. Payton, executive director, Commission on Religion and Race, National Council of Churches. These inspirational and challenging addresses set the stage for the departmental meetings which followed.

The last convention of the Palmetto Education Association was held on March 9 and 10, 1967. Executive Secretary Solomon, in his report to the House of Delegates on March 4, 1967, gave this description of the plans for the last annual convention:

> On Thursday night we will have Governor McNair and State Superintendent of Education, Dr. Busbee. We invited the Governor because he has supported our educational goals for South Carolina. He agreed, in a conference with Allen Williams and yours truly, that he would support free textbooks, compulsory school attendance law, reduced pupil-teacher ratio, and more money for individual school needs. The Governor repeated these promises in a conference with C. E. Watkins and Mr. David Belton, Execuive Secretary of the South Carolina Congress of Parents and Teachers. You have heard and read of Dr. Busbee's comments on the compulsory school attendance law. Because of the support these individuals are giving us in educational goals we advocate, we thought it only appropriate and fitting to invite them to address our convention. Friday morning, Dr. Applegate, president of the National Education Association, will speak. Friday evening we will have a panel, Mrs. Elizabeth D. Koontz, immediate past president of N.E.A. Department of Classroom Teachers and a candidate for president-elect of the N.E.A.; M. T. Puryear, Associate Executive Director of the National Urban League; and Senator George Hanley, Kansas City. Departmental meetings will be held on Thursday and Friday afternoons.[10]

As we take a retrospective look at these conventions over the years, it becomes more obvious than ever that they played an important role in building a strong professional organization for our time. The general sessions were expected to provide inspiration and intellectual stimulation. This they did in a very impressive way.

CHAPTER XI

The Departments Undergird Professional Growth

Hold every man a debtor to his profession.

Francis Bacon

The *State Teachers Association Bulletin* published in March 1920 provides a record of the meetings of the departments of the Association. They were referred to as "group meetings," but they were the forerunners of the departments. The names of the groups and the presiding officers were the following: College Presidents, Dr. R. S. Wilkinson; School Principals, Professor S. L. Finley; College Professors, Professor W. D. Prince; High School Teachers, Mrs. C. B. McWhirter; Teachers in the Intermediate Grades, Mrs. B. A. Sawyer; and Teachers in Primary Grades, Mrs. S. Benjamin.

There was also a special meeting of Jeanes Teachers with J. B. Felton, state agent for Negro schools, presiding.[1]

The by-laws of the new constitution adopted in 1923 provided for 11 departments: Colleges and Secondary Schools, Primary Teachers, Grammar Grade Teachers, School Principals and Supervisors, Teachers of English, Teachers of Science and Mathematics, Language Teachers, Teachers of Education, Vocational Education, History Teachers, and Home Economics.[2]

The November 1923 issue of the *Bulletin* published the first written reports of the departmental meetings held in April 1923. The Department of History Teachers had a very extensive report. Other departments reporting were the Principals, the Jeanes Supervisors, the Smith–Hughes Teachers of Agriculture, and the Teach-

171

ers of Education. As early as 1923 the value of these departmental meetings was emphasized. One of the recommendations made by the Department of Teachers of Education was "that these group meetings receive more emphasis annually, that is, that more time should be given to all of the group meetings, as they are by far the most profitable of the sessions."[3]

The 11 departments provided by the by-laws were never fully established because some groups were combined that should have been separated and other teacher groups were not included. For example, Colleges and Secondary Schools should have constituted two departments rather than one, and some provision should have been made for rural teachers and Jeanes Supervisors.

During the twenties the following persons provided most of the leadership for the departmental groups: Primary Teachers—Miss B. H. Beaumont, Miss Helen Usher, Miss Ruth Bynum; Elementary Teachers—Mrs. L. A. Cain, Mrs. Elsie C. Nelson; English Teachers—Dean Henry Pearson, Miss Thomasena Thomas; Science Teachers—T. L. Duckett; History Teachers—F. C. Redfern, Mrs. C. D. Saxon; Home Economics Teachers—Miss M. M. Fitzgerald, Miss Dora Boston; Vocational Agriculture Teachers—J. S. Shanklin; Smith–Hughes Teachers—J. P. Burgess; Jeanes Teachers—U. S. Gallman, Mrs. A. M. Garrett; Education Teachers—J. T. Williamson; Principals—J. L. Cain, S. L. Finley; and College Teachers—R. S. Wilkinson, D. H. Sims.

From 1923 to 1935 each department planned and presented its own program. There was no convention theme to guide the groups in their planning. Consequently, there was little if any coordination of programs. Each functioned as a separate entity, and the attendance depended upon the ability of the leaders to present meaningful programs for the teachers in their particular group. As the leadership changed, there were some groups which either did not meet or made no reports of their meetings.[4] In the early thirties the interest in departmental meetings was decreasing; and the leaders of the Association, especially A. A. Sims, expressed deep concern about this aspect of the Association's program.

By 1935 there was a reawakening of the departments motivated by the selection of a theme for the convention program. Each department was asked to plan its program to relate to the theme—"Training for Character and Citizenship." As a result of this action by the program planners of the convention, the following changes were made in the departments: (1) the College Department was reactivated; (2) a new Department of Rural Teachers was organized; (3) the trade teachers were reorganized; and (4) special reports were submitted by the Vocational Agriculture, Home Economics, and AVA groups.

There were two other developments during this time which deserve special mention. The elementary school teachers organized an urban group for teachers in city schools (the rural teachers already had a separate department), and the History Department was reactivated with a special focus on Negro history.

A department for English teachers and another for mathematics teachers were reestablished in 1937; and in 1938, the Science Department was reactivated. In 1939, two new departments were added —one for librarians and another for Works Progress Administration (WPA) teachers to expand the government's program of adult education. It is also significant to note that this was the year that the home economics teachers and teachers of agriculture held their first joint meeting.

This reawakening of interest in the departmental meetings during the latter half of the thirties may also be attributed to the leadership of K. W. Green, on the college level; Mrs. S. S. Rice and Mrs. Ida Green, with rural teachers; Mrs. Etta B. Rowe and Miss Rosamond Alston, with urban elementary teachers; M. A. Entzminger and H. V. Harper, with trade teachers; Miss Mary R. Saxon and F. C. Hipp, with mathematics teachers; L. F. Buckner, with science teachers; Miss M. A. Broadnax and Miss Hilda Grayson, with history teachers; Mrs. Charliese P. Sheffield, with librarians; and Mrs. Dora Daniels, with WPA teachers.

THE 1940's: NEW EXPANSION AND LEADERSHIP

During the decade of the forties there were some changes in the leadership of the old departments. Some of the new chairpersons were Miss Fannie Cassell and Miss Hattie Dingle in the primary department, Zack Townsend in mathematics, and H. C. McLendon in science. In the elementary department Mrs. E. E. Riley and Mrs. Pauline Carter served as chairpersons, and the rural teachers group was chaired by Mrs. Corine White and Mrs. Justine Washington. The chairpersons of the library group during this period were Mrs. A. R. Nix, Mrs. Etta Washington, and Miss Emily Copeland. J. E. Beck was chairperson of the principals and the high school teachers had Mrs. Harriett Rogers and Mr. Eugene Hunt as their leaders. The chairpersons of the industrial teachers were Paul Stewart and John R. Harper; and Eugene Barnwell, Gabe Buckman, and W. F. Hickson were the leaders of the agriculture teachers.

In addition to these leadership changes from 1940 to 1950, five new departments were added. In 1948, Fine Arts Education with Mrs. E. J. Southern as chairperson and Health, Physical Education, and Recreation chaired by Thomas Martin were added to the Association's departments. In 1949, a Negro History Department was carved out of the Social Science Department with Mrs. Hilda Grayson Finney serving as its first chairperson. The Social Science Department continued under the leadership of Mrs. Thelma Fields. During the same year a Religious Education Department with the Reverend C. H. Brown as chairperson became a part of the Association's program; and the South Carolina Future Teachers of America, with Miss Trudelle Wimbush as its sponsor, also became a department.

It is significant to note the resurgence of vitality in the departmental groups throughout the last three years of the decade of the forties. As has already been pointed out, the first six years of this period were very difficult indeed. World War II and other problems stemming from educational inequalities had a very debilitating effect upon the Association and was reflected in the departmental meetings. The reawakening of interest during the latter half of the thirties had diminished, and all of the departments needed to be revived again.

This was done in several ways: (1) the executive secretary contacted every leader or chairperson in the fall after the Program Committee made its report and assisted them in preparing for the departmental meetings; (2) each department was given a budget to underwrite its operational expenses; and (3) consultants and resource persons were made available to the departments.

By way of comparison, the Association spent $2,693 for annual operation in 1941 compared to $17,896 in 1948. The total income in 1941 was $6,058 compared to $20,183 in 1945. More money was spent by the Association for the professional improvement of its members.

In his annual message to the convention on March 24, 1949, President Potts made this reference to the professional growth the departments were stimulating:

> Now let us consider what our Association has done to elevate our professional standards and stimulate professional growth. It is in this area that I believe we have made the most progress. Many of you remember the time when our group meetings were very poorly attended because politics had a greater appeal than professonal growth. It is also true that many of our teachers looked upon the two days given them to attend the convention as holidays and came to Columbia merely to have a good time and parade their spring outfits. However, since the Association decided to spend more money for professional growth and secured outstanding persons to serve as consultants for our various groups, the rooms are too small to hold the numbers of teachers who attend. Now our Association is more of an institute than an Easter Parade. Our teachers are seriously trying to improve themselves rather than waste their time with frivolity.[5]

GROWTH IN THE 1950's

The departments of the Palmetto State Teachers Association continued to stimulate professional growth among its members during the decade of the fifties. The number of departments increased from six in 1923 to twenty-one in 1951.

The *Journal of the Palmetto State Teachers Association* of March 1951 lists the groups and chairpersons as follows: Primary Education, Mrs. Robbie Wright; Intermediate Education, W. T. Pleasant; Secondary School Education, Eugene Hunt; Elementary Principals, J. A. Miller; Secondary Principals, W. G. Nichols; College and Higher Education, H. D. Gregg; Bandmasters, Reginald Thomasson; Health, Physical Education, and Recreation, W. T. Green; Library Science, Mrs. W. E. Johnson; Rural Education, Mrs. Corine White; Agriculture, Gabe Buckman; Home Economics, Miss Florine Cooper; American Vocational Education, H. W. Crawford; Fine Arts Education, Mrs. Edith DeVane; Jeanes Teachers, Miss Floy O. Mitchum; English Teachers, R. P. Greene; Business Education, Miss Cora Simpson; Negro History, Mrs. Hilda Finney; Religious Education, the Reverend Warren Jenkins; Future Teachers of America, Miss Trudelle Wimbush.

During the next year (1952), the entire departmental structure of the Palmetto State Teachers Association was reorganized to provide separate departments for the Palmetto State Teachers Association, the secondary schools, and the elementary schools.[6]

The PSTA departments were Secondary Principals, Elementary Principals, Future Teachers of America, Jeanes Teachers, and County Presidents. The elementary school departments were Primary, Lower Intermediate, and Upper Intermediate Grades. All of the other departmental groups were placed in the category of secondary schools. This reorganization gave all of these departments permanent status with the Palmetto State Teachers Association. The chairpersons of these departments met in October of each year, after the Convention Planning Committee made its report, to plan for the professional growth of the members. This arrangement gave the state association a stronger voice in the professional improvement of its teachers and, at the same time, gave the teachers the assurance of the involvement and support of the Palmetto State Teachers Association. One of the reasons for having the planning meeting in October was to give the Planning Committee enough time to make its report to the Executive Committee. After the Executive Committee approved the dates, the main speakers, the theme, and the specific budgets, the departmental chairpersons had the information needed to plan for departmental meetings.

Jeanes Teachers Conference, 1952.

Between 1951 and 1960 nine departments were added to the Association's program: 1951—County Presidents, H. H. Marshall; Elementary School Principals, J. A. Miller; Business Education, Miss Cora Simpson. 1952—Audio-Visual Aids, W. E. Johnson. 1953—Driver Education, L. M. Fair. 1954—Council of Higher Education, Howard Jordan. 1955—Pupil Personnel and Guidance, J. C. Tingman. 1956—Special Education, Mrs. L. B. Smith; Classroom Teachers, H. L. Barksdale.

Organizing the Department of Classroom Teachers was a very significant achievement in that it gave added strength to the Palmetto Education Association and National Education Association by promoting the establishment of high standards of professional ethics, ideas, and loyalty.

ADDITIONS IN THE 1960's

Between 1960 and 1963, five departments were added to the Association. They were, including chairpersons: Retired Teachers, J. E. Blanton; Adult Education, L. L. Pendarvis; Foreign Languages, Mrs. Mary A. Morgan; Art, David R. Clark; and Council for Exceptional Children, W. C. Searls.

On November 23, 1963, the executive committees of the Departments of Primary and Intermediate Education met for the purpose of discussing the need for more departmental offerings at the primary and intermediate levels. It was agreed that there should be more subject matter areas in these two departments.[7] In the Intermediate Department, guidance, mathematics, physical education, and science were established as separate areas; and arithmetic, communication arts, and music were chosen as special areas in the Primary Department.[8]

By 1965 the demand for more professional growth through the expansion of departmental groups had grown so great that the Palmetto Education Association had to increase the number of such groups to 36. The size and the number of the departments created an urgent need for larger and additional physical facilities. There were no facilities within walking distance of the Convention Center at the Township Auditorium. Consequently, it became necessary to operate shuttle busses from the auditorium to Booker T. Washington,

The South Carolina Secondary Schools Activities Association

C. A. Johnson, and Carver schools. The city Chamber of Commerce provided this service for the Palmetto Education Association one year.

SPECIAL DEPARTMENTAL PROJECTS

No description of the importance of these departmental meetings would be complete without referring to the special projects of some of the departmental groups.

In 1954, the Department of Secondary School Principals organized the South Carolina Secondary School Activities Association (SCSSAA). Already referred to in Chapter V, this action produced such good results in regulating and stimulating athletic, cultural, and scholastic activities in the high schools of the state that it merits additional comments.

Three years later, in 1957, the Natural Science Division under the chairmanship of J. Michael Graves conducted for the first time a Science Fair among the junior and senior high schools of the state. This fair stimulated students to use their initiative and creativity in developing projects in mathematics, chemistry, biology, and physics. Annually, for a period of eleven years, two of the top winners participated in the National Science Fair. In five of those eleven years, South Carolina Negro schools had a national winner.

In 1961, the Department of Elementary School Principals held its first spelling bee. There was a district elimination contest followed by a state contest to be held between April 15 and 30. Any pupil below the seventh grade who had not reached age 13 by May 1 was eligible to compete. The rules for the state spelling bee may be found in the September 1961 issue of the *Palmetto Education Association Journal.*[9]

1966: DEPARTMENTS AND THEIR CHAIRPERSONS

So many people contributed so much to strengthen the departments of their choice that it will be impossible to give all of them the commendation they deserve for their unselfish and voluntary service. Some mention has been made of those who provided the leadership when the first departments were organized. Others have been mentioned as new departments were added.

This chapter closes with a listing of those who were in departmental leadership positions in 1966 as the Association was in the process of merging with the South Carolina Education Association: Agriculture, Frank Adams, Jr.; American Vocational Association, J. R. Taylor; Adult Education, L. L. Pendarvis; Art, Sylvester L. Mills; Bandmasters, Harold H. June; Business Education, Mrs. V. D. Senior; Classroom Teachers, Mrs. Mamie Coker; Council for Exceptional Children, Mrs. Joyce N. Long; Driver Education, James J. McCray; Elementary Principals, Boyd W. Tyler; English, Gibbs A. Dozier; Foreign Languages, Mrs. Peggy Mitchell; Guidance, James D. Kibler; Health, Physical Education, and Recreation, Kenneth Sandiford; Higher Education, John F. Potts; Home Economics, Mrs. S. T. Mims; Guidance Division for Intermediate Grades, Mrs. Janie Kershaw; Modern Math Division of Intermediate Grades, Mrs. Rosa Wilds; Physical Education Division of Intermediate Grades, Miss Nellie Gordon; Reading Division of Intermediate Grades, Miss M. Seawright; Science Division of Intermediate Grades, Mrs. W. J. Hallman; Social Studies Division of Intermediate Grades, Mrs. Amarintha Wright; Librarians, Miss M. F. Griffin; Mathematics, W. D. Young; Music Education, James Williams; Natural Sciences, Rodney Albert; Communication Arts Division of Primary Grades, Mrs. Mary P. Grainger; Fine Arts Division of Primary Grades, Mrs. L. S. Rainey;

Physical Education Division of Primary Grades, Mrs. S. W. Reynolds; Social Sciences Division of Primary Grades, Mrs. A. A. Harrell; Religious Education, the Reverend G. A. Thomas; Retired Teachers, Mrs. Albertha J. Murray; Secondary Principals, A. R. Rucker; Social Studies, Mrs. Fannie S. Ivey; Supervisors and Consultants, Mrs. Evelyn B. Haynes; and Trade and Industrial Education, D. L. Barno, Jr.[10]

Tracing the birth and growth of the departments of the Association from 1920 to 1966 makes obvious the tremendous impact they had upon the professional growth of Negro teachers in South Carolina. Without the influence and stimulation of these departments, teacher competence would not have improved as much as it did, and pupil performance may not have risen.

CHAPTER XII

Affiliations With Other Professional Organizations

All your strength is in your union.

Henry Wadsworth Longfellow

The earliest record of any contact of the American Teachers Association (ATA), formerly the National Association of Teachers in Colored Schools (NATCS), with Negro teachers in South Carolina was in August 1919 when its annual convention was held at South Carolina State College in Orangeburg. Dean N. C. Nix commented on this convention as follows: "The National Association of Teachers in Colored Schools held their annual convention at the State Agricultural and Mechanical School July 31–August 3, 1919. Eminent educators from all parts of the United States attended the sessions."[1]

PSTA DELEGATES TO ATA, FORMERLY NATCS

The invitation to hold this convention in Orangeburg with South Carolina State College as host was extended by President Robert S. Wilkinson. The Chamber of Commerce of the City of Orangeburg donated $260 to assist in defraying the expenses. One of the important results of this convention was the stimulation of interest of Negro teachers in South Carolina in NATCS. The financial statement for 1921 shows a travel expense item of $160 for a delegate to the NATCS convention in Oklahoma City, Oklahoma, but there

181

is no mention of the name of the delegate.[2] The financial report for 1922 did not have an expense item for travel to Hampton Institute where the next convention was held. However, the Palmetto State Teachers Association did send a contribution of $10 to the national organization, indicating its continued interest. In 1923 President R. W. Mance appointed J. T. Williamson, professor of education at State A and M College, as the delegate to NATCS from the PSTA. After attending the twentieth annual convention on July 25–27, 1923, Professor Williamson wrote the first report ever to appear in the *Bulletin*.

> There were upward to 600 delegates and visitors present at the meeting, numbering some of the most prominent educators working among our group. All delegates to the meeting were entertained as guests of the Tuskeegee Institution—no charges being made for their accommodation. The welcome address was delivered by Mr. Warren Logan, Vice Principal of the Institute. This was most ably responded to by Mrs. Bethune. In his annual address, Dr. John A. Gregg reveiwed the "Progress of Negro Education" and suggested the slogan, "No illiteracy by 1930" to be adopted by the association and urged the members to put forth every effort to attain this goal. "Vitalizing Education" was the conference theme.[3]

C. A. Johnson, vice-president of PSTA, was the delegate to NATCS in 1925. His report was printed in full in the March 1926 issue of the *Bulletin*.[4] In 1927, Mr. Johnson was appointed by W. A. Robinson, president of the NATCS, to a special committee to seek National Education Association assistance in having Negro high schools accredited. This blue ribbon committee consisted of H. C. Trenholm, Mrs. Mary McLeod Bethune, Dr. John N. Gandy, Dr. J. E. Shepherd, Garnett C. Wilkinson, and Dr. N. B. Young. Mrs. Thelma D. Perry, author of *The History of the American Teachers Association,* made this significant statement:

> One dominant problem which concerned Trenholm, Robinson and all of the other Negro educators by the mid-twenties, was accreditation of their schools, particularly the high schools. Pupils from unaccredited schools were not eligible to enter first rate colleges, and where they were admitted it was on a disadvantaged basis. This was a major consideration, though not the only one, which prompted the efforts of NATCS to establish a working relationship with NEA.[5]

The PSTA had a special interest in the accrediting of Negro high schools because a study was made in 1925–26 to determine the number of accredited Negro high schools in the 16 southern states with separate schools, and South Carolina had none. At that time there were 5,140 accredited high schools in 15 states (South Carolina did not reply to this inquiry) for white pupils and only 204 for Negroes.[6] This issue alone was important enough to attract the attention and secure the cooperation of the leaders of the PSTA.

After 1926 all delegates to the NATCS were elected by the convention rather than appointed by the president. The Executive Committee recommended this change, and the body approved it. The first person to be elected to represent the PSTA at the NATCS convention in 1927 was Mrs. Alice E. Webb of Anderson. Her election was unanimous. Mrs. Webb was very active in the affairs of the Association and served for a number of years on the Executive Committee from the Third District. H. D. Gregg, dean of Claflin College, was elected in 1928 as the representative to the NATCS.

In 1930, President A. A. Sims recommended that "the Association become affiliated with the National Teachers Association (American Teachers Association) and send a delegate yearly to attend the meetings of the body."[7] Each year since 1930 the Asociation has sent one or two delegates and made a substantial contribution to the work of the national organization.

During the next decade this interest in the ATA was greatly stimulated by the report of the delegates to the ATA conventions and also by the ATA representatives who were sent to the annual conventions of the Association. Some of the most influential members of the PSTA were elected as delegates. W. A. Perry and Miss Laura Hill were elected to serve as delegates in 1930. By 1936 the number of delegates elected by the Association increased to five. They were Mrs. Ida Green, Mrs. Alice La Saine, M. F. Whittaker, H. B. Rikard, and S. L. Finley. Other members from South Carolina in attendance were J. P. Burgess, W. W. Wilkins, E. E. Riley, and J. S. Shanklin. C. A. Johnson was reelected in his absence to the position of regional vice-president of ATA.[8]

C. V. Bing, who was president of the Association at this time (1936), recommended in his annual address to the convention that "this body continue its efforts toward building strong sentiment in the state for the National Association. This body is pursuing a far-reaching program, and with proper support, good is sure to result. The ultimate objectives of this body cannot obtain unless the several states stand solidly behind its efforts."[9]

President Bing also recommended that a membership drive be conducted in all counties in the state for the purpose of increasing the membership of South Carolina teachers in the ATA. As a matter of fact, every president during the thirties, from A. A. Sims to G. A. Anderson, strongly supported the ATA and urged more PSTA members to enroll and actively participate in its program.

The problems that the PSTA experienced from 1940 to 1946 did not diminish its interest in nor its support of the ATA. As a matter of fact, there was a greater need for closer cooperation to broaden the base of support for equalization of educational facilities and expenditures. It was also felt that a stronger appeal for federal aid to education could be made through the combined efforts of all states with segregated schools than with one state working alone. In addition, the ATA was working with the NEA on the critical problem of accreditation. This had a special appeal to the leaders of the PSTA. As a result of these special needs and the untiring efforts of Presidents Mims, Gallman, McCain, and Potts, the executive secretary, and many others who served as delegates, there was a tremendous increase in memberships in ATA by PSTA members. During this period John F. Potts was elected regional vice-president, and Frank De Costa and Guerney Nelson, Sr. were elected state directors. South Carolina moved from the third state from the bottom in membership to the third state from the top. By 1950 the memberships were large enough to have South Carolina qualify for 21 delegates. The minutes of the April 7, 1950 meeting record this account of the action taken:

> According to the previous year's membership, the PSTA is entitled to 21 representatives. Following some discussion a motion was made by Mr. I. N. R. Harper, seconded by Reverend J. W. Shaw, that a bus be chartered from Columbia to Montgomery and carry the allotted delegation who will assume their own expenses at the convention. Mr. McLester stated an unreadiness in the form of a substitute motion that such be, provided the amount required does not exceed the amount allotted in the budget for that purpose. Mr. D. G. Cureton offered a substitute to the substitute that the amount

expended for the bus should not exceed $300. The motion was passed by a vote of 54 to 3. Mr. A. T. Butler then moved, seconded by President Potts, that each of the six Congressional Districts be allowed three delegates and that the remainder of the delegation consist of state officers, ATA officers and members of the Program Committee. The motion carried.[10]

This was the beginning of the annual bus trip to the ATA convention by members of the PEA and was continued until ATA merged with NEA in 1966. It was a special summer event which all delegates looked forward to with very pleasant anticipation.

After 1950 the delegates to the ATA (except state officers) were elected by the six congressional districts. Each district was at first permitted to send only three representatives, but as more PEA members joined the ATA, the state could qualify for more delegates. Each state was permitted one delegate for every twenty-five members. By 1955 the PEA increased the district's delegates to six. At that time the PEA had over 1,600 members in the ATA.

In 1953 the ATA met again in Orangeburg, South Carolina, and Gerard A. Anderson, a former PEA president, was unanimously elected president. He previously served two years as vice-president.

Another PEA member, Clinton Young of Charleston, was elected vice-president of ATA at the 1955 convention. Four years later in 1959, Leila Bradby, another former president of PEA, was elected vice-president of ATA; and in 1960 she was elected to the presidency of this organization. Still another PEA president, H. L. Barksdale, was elected vice-president of ATA in 1965.

After 1955 when the PEA memberships in the ATA increased to more than 1,600, the number of delegates from South Carolina ranged from 30 to 50 every year. By 1965, the membership in ATA increased to an all-time high of 4,360. Until the merger with the NEA became a reality, the ATA continued to receive very solid support from the teachers of South Carolina.

NATIONAL EDUCATION ASSOCIATION AFFILIATION

On March 29, 1947 the House of Delegates held a meeting at Allen University. At that time "Mr. S. L. Finley made a motion that

Mr. A. T. Butler, our Executive Secretary, be elected as our delegate to the National Education Association. The motion was seconded by Reverend Brewer. The motion carried."[11]

This motion made by Mr. Finley was the beginning of the PEA's affiliation with the NEA. When Mr. Butler made his report to the House of Delegates on November 22, 1947, he emphasized these four points:

> It was the first time in the history of the NEA that a Negro has been included in the South Carolina delegation.
>
> Representation at the NEA Convention is based upon one delegate per 500 members.
>
> It is important that more teachers join the NEA in order that we would always have representation in this national organzation.
>
> The organization is pushing for federal aid. Because of conditions in the South, this section of the country would be aided more than the other sections, hence another reason for increased membership.[12]

Mr. David Stoney, president of the state chapter of the NEA, said that the most significant contribution made at the NEA Convention from South Carolina came from Mr. Butler.

The following year (1948), J. B. Beck and I. C. Wiley were elected as delegates to the NEA. However, it was not until 1951 that the PEA actually became an affiliate of the NEA because there were not enough memberships in the national organization to qualify. At that time the first bonafide delegates were sent to the San Francisco Convention. These delegates were J. C. Parler and W. E. Solomon. In 1952 the PEA membership increased enough to qualify for four delegates. The House elected Carl Fields, W. E. Solomon, Aaron Rucker, and James Miller. There were 11 South Carolina teachers in attendance at this convention. The other seven probably represented counties which would qualify if they had 100 members in the NEA or visited as non-delegates.

The citation given to Mrs. Eloise Key Pendarvis for becoming the five hundred thousandth teacher enrolled in the NEA stimulated the membership campaign in South Carolina for the NEA. In 1953 the Association qualified for seven delegates (three more than the year before), and by 1958 the number of delegates had increased to twenty.[13]

In 1959 the number of delegates to the NEA convention was 24. Of this number, 16 were delegates from county associations which were affiliated with the NEA. By 1962, the delegates from the PEA increased to 45, with 38 representing counties in South Carolina. The total membership of PEA teachers in the NEA increased from less than 500 in 1951, the date of affiliation, to 6,217 in 1967. This is not only phenomenal growth in numbers, but it is an excellent indication of the outstanding professional stimulation the PEA provided for its members.

STRENGTH IN AFFILIATION

This affiliation with these professional organizations was a tremendous source of strength to the PEA. Without the much needed services which they rendered and the influence they wielded because of their size and prestige, it is doubtful that the PEA would have become a potent force in the equalizing of educational opportunities or desegregating public education. The ATA provided a special kind of assistance that could not have been obtained from any other source. It was dealing with the same problems confronting South Carolina's Negro teachers—elimination of discrimination in education, compulsory school attendance, and federal aid to education. Consequently, the PEA supported to the fullest extent the objectives it adopted. Some of the most significant were as follows:

1. Equality of opportunity for every child and equal professional status for every teacher. After the 1954 decision of the United States Supreme Court, the emphasis was focused upon the orderly processes of desegregation.

2. The elimination of flagrant abuses in education through the NAACP Educational and Legal Defense Fund. For a period of 15 years from 1940 to 1955, the ATA contributed one-tenth of its annual membership income to this fund. By 1955 this amounted to $19,000.[14]

3. The improvement of the image of minority groups in textbooks used in the nation's classrooms. A textbook review commission was set up for this purpose.

4. Support of federal aid to education.

When ATA merged with NEA in 1966, there was no longer a need for the joint NEA–ATA committee to deal with problems of mutual concern. Most of the objectives of ATA had already been discussed by this joint committee, and most of the unrealized objectives were accepted by the NEA as one of its obligations. For example, in the one hundred first annual convention in 1963, two of the three overriding topics were civil rights and federal support for education.

These two professional organizations made a salutory impact on the PEA and contributed significantly to its growth and development.

CHAPTER XIII

Protecting the Rights of Teachers

... in the field of public education the doctrine of "separate but equal" had no place. Separate educational facilities are inherently unequal.

> Chief Justice Earl Warren,
> U.S. Supreme Court
> Brown vs. Board of
> Education of Topeka, 1954

The Association's concern for teachers passed through three stages of emphasis: better teacher preparation, salary equalization, and improving the welfare and protecting the rights of teachers.

When it was discovered that Negro teachers were poorly qualified, the Association attempted to improve their preparation by making grants to summer institutes which were organized for this purpose, and the four-year colleges were urged to give this critical matter very high priority. In 1926, a survey was made of the Negro teachers (See Chapter II) revealing that only 64 of the 699 applicants who took the teachers examination qualified for certificates. Not one of the 64 met the qualifications for a first grade certificate; all of them received second grade certificates. This deplorable situation was called to the attention of the Negro teacher training institutions in the state, and in 11 years (1926–1937) 76 percent of the Negro teachers earned first grade certificates. Twenty-two percent held second grade certificates, and only two percent fell below second grade qualifications. The Palmetto State Teachers Association also improved instructional methods and procedures through the various subject matter groups or departments which it sponsored. Special

189

emphasis was placed on methodology as well as subject matter content. Numerous demonstrations were arranged to show how the practical is linked to the theoretical. From its earliest inception, the Association has put forth special efforts to realize one of its basic purposes—"the improvement of its members in the science and art of teaching."[1]

After significant progress was made in the preparation of teachers, the second stage requiring special attention was higher remuneration for their work. The better-prepared teachers were being lured away to other states with higher salary scales. Others were leaving the profession for more lucrative positions in other fields. This disturbing situation was called to the attention of the state Department of Education and the state superintendent during each administration but to no avail. Then the need for higher salaries for Negro teachers was carried to the governor and the state legislature by ad hoc and legislative committees of the Association. These efforts also brought no favorable responses. In desperation, an open letter was sent to influential citizens and the news media in an attempt to get community support. Some favorable replies were received, but nothing substantial was done to increase the teachers' salaries. It soon became quite evident that these special appeals were not producing results and that a new strategy was needed.

"In the early 1940's the NAACP initiated a nationwide effort to improve the salaries of teachers in schools for Negro children."[2] Collaboration with the NAACP appeared to be the only possible way to get the desired results. Consequently, the leaders of the Association and the NAACP through a joint committee of both organizations planned the legal procedures. The main thrust of the litigation became *equalizing* rather than *raising* salaries.

The first step in this joint effort was taken by the Palmetto State Teachers Association in 1942 when on December 31 of that year the Executive Committee authorized Mrs. Ida Green, the treasurer, to set aside $1,200 for a Defense Fund.[3] The House of Delegates had previously adopted a resolution in April 1941 to start equalization of salaries in 1941–42 and complete it in two years. However, it was delayed much longer because of the opposition of some of the members of the House of Delegates to court action. The sequence of events leading up to the motion that authorized joint action and use of Defense Fund money may be found in Chapter III.

In 1945, the Association cooperated with the state conference of the NAACP and provided financial assistance for the filing of two suits to equalize salaries. One was filed by Miss Duvall, a teacher in Charleston, South Carolina. The other suit was filed by Mr. Thompson, a Columbia, South Carolina teacher. These court suits "spearheaded equalization of salaries by the State and the equalization of salary supplements by some districts."[4] However, the state Department of Education devised a new teacher certification system which required the National Teachers Examination as a major criteria for certification and salary. The state legislature enacted into law a new proposed state aid salary schedule which based all teachers' salaries (Negro and white) on training, experience, and the score on the National Teachers Examination. The House of Delegates unanimously adopted this schedule on November 30, 1946 (see Chapter IV). The adoption of this new state aid salary schedule helped in solving the problem of equalizing salaries, but it created another critical problem for the Association—preparing Negro teachers to meet the new and higher qualifications for certification. Since most of the Negro teachers were products of separate but unequal school systems and had little if any access to graduate training, they could not qualify for the higher paying certificates. The Association placed this matter high on its agenda and provided seminars, workshops, and institutes to help teachers acquire the necessary qualifications. The Negro colleges, especially South Carolina State through its summer and graduate schools and extension centers, also played a significant role in the preparation of teachers for recertification. The Allen–Benedict Summer School also responded to this need.

The third stage through which the Association passed was to improve the welfare and protect the rights of its members. After the goal of salary equalization was realized with the assistance of the NAACP, the Association continued to set aside funds for the purpose of filing other suits in the future to protect the rights of teachers. To provide this protection, it was necessary to maintain a continuous cooperative relationship with the NAACP. The NAACP sent a representative to the meetings of the House of Delegates to give progress reports of plans made and actions taken. Even more important was the decision to keep earmarking funds to underwrite the costs of court action. By 1948 the Defense Fund had increased to $3,500.

The first report of the committee appointed to work with the NAACP was made to the House of Delegates on April 5, 1946 at Allen University. Three main items of business were discussed in the first meeting of the joint committee on May 6, 1945:

1. A report of the Thompson trial. At that time the trial was over, but the judge had not handed down a decision.

2. A report of expenditures of the trial which amounted to $1,055. This did not include the $500 to be paid to Mr. Thompson if the case caused him to lose his teaching position.

3. A motion to enter a suit for equality in graduate and professional education.[5]

Another report of this committee was made to the House of Delegates on March 27, 1947. The minutes of that meeting provide this account:

> Mr. N. R. Harper then made the report for the Joint Committee of the House of Delegates and the N.A.A.C.P. He read a letter from Mr. Hinton in which a request was made for $500.00 to be granted to the N.A.A.C.P. by the P.S.T.A. for the transportation case. In the same letter there was a request for $500.00 to help pay the expenses of a Law Suit brought by John Wrighten against the University of South Carolina. There was considerable discussion over which case took precedence over the other. After Rev. H. B. Butler explained the situation very clearly, the body voted the first $500 for the suit which was brought by Mr. John Wrighten against the University of South Carolina to enter the Law School. Mr. Madden made the motion, Mr. Sharper seconded. The motion was carried.
>
> Rev. C. H. Brown then made the motion that an additional $500.00 be granted the N.A.A.C.P. for the transportation case which they were planning in order to provide better transportation for Negro children. Rev. Sharper seconded the motion. The motion was carried.[6]

After the first three court suits brought by the NAACP with the assistance of the PSTA were successful, there was less opposition to this cooperative arrangement among the members of the Association. Funds were voted for court action by the NAACP whenever they were requested. James M. Hinton spoke to the House of Delegates on March 25, 1948 and reported for the Joint Committee. He reviewed "the February 1944 Charleston Suit, the 1945 Columbia Suit and the July 1947 Wrighten Case"[7] and stated that the Committee was launching a third phase—a transportation suit. Following this report the House of Delegates immediately earmarked an additional $1,000 for this lawsuit.

TEACHER WELFARE FUND: PROTECTION OF RIGHTS AND JOB SECURITY

While these victories in court gained more support from the Negro teachers, they increased the opposition of the segregationists within and without the teaching profession. Efforts to intimidate and dismiss teachers who supported or initiated suits were stepped up, and special efforts were made to find out which teachers held membership in the NAACP. It then became more imperative than ever to protect the rights of those teachers who were supporting the organization bringing the court suits.

In 1951, the Association accepted the recommendation of Executive Secretary Solomon to establish a teacher welfare fund. This money would be used to get legal interpretation of school laws and aid teachers who were flagrantly abused or unfairly dismissed from their positions. This welfare fund and the Defense Fund already referred to served the same basic purpose of equalizing salaries, facilities, and services. However, the welfare fund was specifically focused upon the protection of the rights of teachers and giving them more job security. It should also be pointed out that the money for the defense funds was earmarked but maintained in the treasury of the PSTA until the funds were needed for the suits. After the establishment of the Welfare Fund in 1951, a special fund was created.

This made the special requests of the past unnecessary. The procedure used by the PSTA was a suit-by-suit arrangement rather than a substantial amount of money placed in a special account for a special purpose. A good example of this arrangement may be found in the minutes of the House of Delegates of the April 6, 1950 meeting. Attorney Harold R. Boulware addressed the House at this meeting and gave this information:

Beginning last fall the legal committee has joined with legal counsel to wage the battle against the theory of separate but equal facilities. Petitions have been filed to do away with this theory. School facilities and bus transportation have been asked for. There have been hearings in District No. 22 of Clarendon County and in District No. 13 in Lee County. They expect to go to Court in the near future.

The decision rendered by the Supreme Court in the Sweatt Case will have a bearing on future action. If segregation itself is declared unconstitutional a new line of attack will be followed.[8]

Attorney Boulware also stated:

... the NAACP is in the red for funds in the teacher defense fund and requested the association to take care of the deficiency as it now existed. A motion by President Potts that the House of Delegates go on record as authorizing the Budget Committee to replace the $413 already used and add $500 was seconded by Mr. Clinton Young, Rev. J. W. Shaw and others. Unreadiness was stated in the form of a suggestion that the sum be made a total of $1,000. The change being accepted by Mr. Potts, the motion was carried unanimously.[9]

After 1951 representatives of the NAACP did not have to appear before the House and make specific requests for specific cases. The name of the Defense Fund authorized by the Executive Committee in 1942 was changed to the Teacher Welfare Fund.

Attorney Boulware's April 1950 reference to "a new line of attack" if school segregation became unconstitutional was a harbinger of things to come. In a little more than four years, the Supreme Court on May 17, 1954 declared the separate but equal theory unconstitutional, and this decision ushered in a new dimension of protection which was urgently needed by teachers. Previously teachers were deeply concerned about losing their positions because they used the courts in getting equalization of salaries and facilities. They were also worried about reprisals for having joined the NAACP. Now desegregation in education brought a new problem, namely the reduction in the number of teachers and administrators needed in the public schools.

Negro teachers, principals, and supervisors knew that when the change came many of their jobs would be in jeopardy. Judging from the inequalities and the practices of the past, they would be threatened.

Indeed, in those southern states where these changes were occurring there was evidence of what they feared—loss of teaching positions by Negroes and the abolition of a large number of principalships and supervisory positions previously held by Negroes.

This situation became so serious that joint action by 17 states with segregated systems was necessary.

> In 1955 Mr. Solomon was authorized by the 17 associations of teachers in schools for Negro children to call a meeting to plan for the protection of all teachers in these states. Invited to participate in this conference were the National Education Association, the Southern Regional Council, and the Legal Defense and Educational Fund, Inc. It was agreed that we establish the Teacher Security and Job Information Services as a division of the Legal Defense and Education Fund, Inc. A formula of contributions to the project was developed by the presidents and the executive secretaries of the several associations and approved by Thurgood Marshall, Director Counsel of the Legal Defense and Education Fund, Inc. Two individuals, Dr. John W. Davis and Elwood Chisolm, were employed to work directly with teachers on educational and legal problems. This alliance has continued through the years and the Legal Defense and Education Fund, Inc. and our Association spent many dollars in successful efforts to aid teachers.[10]

THE ELLOREE CASE

One of the efforts of the Association to defend teachers was the action taken on the Elloree teachers' complaint against their superintendent and trustee board. On May 22, 1956, a delegation of teachers from Elloree accompanied by the president of the Orangeburg County Teachers Association met with the PEA Executive Committee to describe some unfavorable actions being taken by their superintendent. They had previously made their appeal for assistance to Executive Secretary Solomon, and he promised to have them present their case to the Executive Committee.

Mr. Davis, serving as spokesman for the group, stated that "they wanted to share information with the Executive Committee with the hope it will help teachers in other communities."[11] He stated further:

> . . . last fall they were given blanks to fill out. There were two questions some objected to. These concerned integration and

N.A.A.C.P. Later each teacher completed the form at the insistence of the Superintendent. During the year they were told by the Board Chairman they would have to think as the Board did if they wanted to return.

This spring they were given another form to fill out. This form had more questions than the previous one.

The teachers in this group notified the Superintendent that they would fill out the form through questions on N.A.A.C.P., but did not want to answer other questions. A request was made for another form. Request refused.

The Superintendent and a trustee came to the school and asked the principal to send teachers into the office in groups of three. They came to the school with the intention of getting the forms signed, and when told by teachers they did not want to fill out the form, they, Superintendent and trustee, stated fill it out or sign a resignation form.[12]

After a lengthy period of questioning by members of the Executive Committee it was decided that a court suit should be filed on behalf of the teachers. The executive secretary then related to the Executive Committee his efforts to determine the eligibility of a suit. He commented on a conversation he had with Directors of the NEA Defense Commission and Commission on Tenure and Academic Freedom. In addition he contacted the American Friends Service Committee and Teacher Security and Job Information Service. "Each organization had expressed concern, requested detailed information (which was forwarded), and indicated violation of Rights of Conscience and Civil Liberties."[13]

Following a period of discussion John R. Bowen made a motion that the Association use its entire resources if necessary for the defense of the teachers. The motion was seconded by H. A. Ashe and others and was passed with the understanding that this action taken by the Executive Committee would have to be approved by the House of Delegates.

Another effort of the PEA to protect the rights of Negro teachers was the filing of a retirement suit to equalize retirement benefits. This was done in collaboration with the NAACP. The attorney for the NAACP was given $500 to file the suit with the understanding that $350 would be refunded if the case did not go to court.[14]

One of the items of the July 20, 1956 meeting of the Executive Committee was a recommendation that a procedure for investigations be established. It was agreed by the members of the committee that "all investigations concerning non-reemployment and abuses of teachers be made by the Executive Secretary with legal and other assistance if necessary. The executive secretary then will report his findings to the Executive Committee. If this committee takes affirmative action, the matter is then referred to the House of Delegates for final action."[15]

On May 16, 1957, Mr. Solomon "reported on the Elloree, Williston, Denmark, and Ruby cases. The Executive Committee instructed him to do whatever possible for the teachers in accordance with Association policies. A motion to furnish NCOSTA funds with which to continue the Elloree Case was approved. In another motion the executive secretary was instructed to write Roundtree that PEA will give any assistance necessary to help him retain his teaching position."[16]

The executive secretary also reported on his efforts to obtain money and moral and legal support for the teachers involved in the cases just mentioned. Some success was realized in that he secured $1,750 for unemployed Elloree teachers, $3,200 for two Elloree teachers who wanted to do graduate work, $300 for the Hutchinson Case, and $1,000 for the Teacher Welfare Fund.

In another report of the executive secretary dated November 2, 1957, he stated that $10,000 was earmarked for the teacher welfare program in 1952 (after his request in 1951) and that $3,600 of that amount was spent over the five-year period. The balance in the fund at the time of this report was $9,229.93.

By 1961 the Teacher Welfare Fund was reduced to $7,396.21. Mr. Solomon called this to the attention of the House of Delegates on January 3, 1961. He stated: "For some time we have not been able to put money into this fund. The increase since the Elloree Case has come from interest earned."[17] He further pointed out that lawyer's fees and court costs have increased and that other Associations have a much larger welfare fund than the PEA.

On October 31, 1964, Executive Secretary Solomon made the following report to the House of Delegates regarding teacher welfare: "In the area of Defense—Welfare, Mr. Moody is out on parole. We plan to file for pardon proceedings at the proper time. The

Rackley Case has been filed. The Williams Case has been filed. These cases will be financed by the Legal Defense Education Fund. There have been many teachers not re-elected over the state. The most recent request we have received was from a case that happened two years ago."[18]

The requests for financial assistance from teachers in South Carolina became so numerous that in 1964 the Association adopted the set of rules that follow.

Rules Governing PEA Defense Welfare Fund

General Rules

1. Assistance from the Fund shall be given in those cases which involve an issue of importance to others of this Association.
2. No assistance will be authorized until careful investigation has been made to determine the nature of the injustice.
3. Investigations shall be conducted by the Association's Executive Secretary and the Chairman of the District in which the aggrieved teacher resides.
4. In processing a case, opinions of the local association officers and the local Professional Rights and Responsibilities Commission will be sought.
5. The Committee for administering the Fund will consist of seven members, five permanent members, and two ad hoc members. The permanent members will be the Executive Secretary, the immediate Past President, the State Chairman of the Professional Rights and Responsibilities Commission, and two Executive Committee members. The two ad hoc members shall be appointed for each specific case by joint action of the P.E.A. President and Executive Secretary. Suggestions for the Two Ad Hoc Members:
   a. President of the local association to which the individual requesting aid belongs.
   b. The local or county Professional Rights and Responsibilities Commission's Chairman.
   c. A person chosen because of special capacities and/or relation to the case involved.
6. The Executive Secretary of the Association will continue correspondence on cases until settlement is made.
7. Any publicity on cases in which assistance is granted shall be given upon advice of the PEA Department Welfare Fund Committee.
8. No names will be used in publicizing cases unless permission is obtained from the individual receiving assistance.
9. All publicity of cases shall be released through the Executive Secretary of PEA.

Legal Cases

1. Requests for financial assistance for legal fees will be processed by the Executive Secretary, the PEA President, the Chairman of the State Professional Rights and Responsibilities Commission and recommendation made to the PEA Executive Committee.
2. Requests for such assistance shall be made prior to the employment of legal counsel by the individual involved.

Cases of Dismissal and Resultant Loss of Salary

1. A PEA member who has been dismissed with loss of salary because of involvement in civil rights movements or whose professional rights have been violated and who is in financial need may receive financial assistance not to exceed one year except in cases involving extraordinary circumstances. In these cases the individual must give evidence of some action being taken to correct the injustice.
2. Requests of this nature will be made to the Executive Secretary and the PEA President and referred to the PEA Defense Welfare Fund Committee.
3. Requests for assistance must be directed to the PEA Defense Welfare Fund Committee in writing. The request must include the reason for dismissal, the salary lost, and evidence of financial need.
4. The amount of assistance is to be determined by present income (at the time of dismissal), size of family, amount of current bills, long term indebtedness, pressing need, number of similar cases being processed at the same time, amount of funds in the Defense Welfare Treasury, and other factors pertinent to the case.
5. Assistance from the Association may be legal and/or financial as determined by the PEA Defense Welfare Committee.[19]

TEACHER DISPLACEMENT DUE TO DESEGREGATION

An NEA task force of southern educators made a survey of the 17 southern and border states in 1965 to ascertain the number of teachers displaced as a result of desegregation. This task force found that faculties in southern schools were often not desegregated when the children were. When all-Negro schools were merged with all-white schools, Negro teachers and administrators were likely to be demoted, to be placed in "limited contact" positions, or to lose their jobs entirely. It is widely assumed by many citizens, in school and out, that Negro teachers and administrators are intellectually inferior and that they cannot provide quality education. The PEA *Journal* reported the following:

In general, the task force reported, the more extensive the desegregation of students, the greater the chances that Negro teachers will be adversely affected by demotion, displacement or dismissal. In many places where Negro schools were closed, although the Negro teachers were dismissed, white teachers with less experience and preparation were employed to take care of the increased number of pupils in the newly integrated schools.[20]

Unfortunately, the Civil Rights Act of 1964 did not provide specific protection for Negro teachers' rights. Consequently, it became even more imperative that the state teachers' association provide this protection for displaced teachers. The problem was becoming more serious every year between 1954 and 1964. There were no overall statistics on the number of Negro teachers who lost their jobs because of desegregation, but Samuel Etheridge, field director of NEA, estimated that as many as 5,500 Negro teachers in the 11 southern states were affected. Scattered reports from the NEA and the NAACP revealed that about 250 teachers definitely lost their jobs in the spring of 1965 because of desegregation. Etheridge further stated that "a far larger number are currently in a kind of limbo, their contracts neither officially terminated nor renewed."[21]

In its June 1965 convention the NEA voted to raise a million dollars to assist displaced southern Negro teachers. There was an informal cooperative arrangement with the NAACP in locating those teachers needing protection and deciding what strategies would provide the best protection for them.

The Commission on Professional Rights and Responsibilities of the PEA strongly supported the Defense—Welfare Committee and endorsed its actions in defending teachers. The purposes of this Commission were as follows:

1. To defend members of the teaching profession, schools, and the cause of education against unjust attacks; to investigate controversies involving teachers and schools justly, fearlessly, and in the public interest.

2. To encourage the development and use of personnel policies that attract and hold competent professional personnel and prevent unnecessary difficulties.

3. To initiate action for legislation that will result in tenure, continuing contracts, or some form of security for teachers.

4. To promote the civil and human rights of members of the teaching profession and foster conditions of academic freedom under which teachers may safely teach the truth without fear or favor.

5. To gather information about various individuals and groups who criticize or oppose education and make resumés of their activities.

6. To investigate cases of alleged unethical conduct by members of the teaching profession when requested to do so by the Executive Committee of the state association.

7. To issue reports and engage in such activities as are appropriate to the development of better understanding by the profession and the public of the areas of concern which are the responsibility of the Commission.[22]

On March 4, 1967 the House of Delegates met at W. A. Perry Junior High School to discuss the merger plan. At that time, attorney Matthew Perry, legal advisor for the Association, made these comments about some of the cases involving the need for protection of teacher rights:

Back in the 1950's the contract of a Charleston teacher was not renewed. We were faced with a principle of law centuries old—school districts have the right to employ, or not to employ, as they see fit—there was no tenure of any kind. Richland county is the exception. Lawyers have long been concerned with helping teachers.

In the 1960's there was much unrest in the state. Some teachers participated and assisted certain committees. This was done at night, giving advice, helping to write statements, etc. Two cases were outstanding, Mrs. Gloria Rackley and Mrs. Irene Williams. These teachers were tops in their profession.

Mrs. Rackley was a member of the N.A.A.C.P. and participated in civil rights activities. Mrs. Irene Williams actively participated in Sumter to the point of carrying a picket sign. The school officials refused to renew Mrs. Williams' contract. Mrs. Rackley's services were terminated October, 1963. In each instance we brought action against a long-standing law and won both cases. The court enjoined school officials from interfering, and Mrs. Williams got her job and back salary. In the Rackley case the school board was enjoined from withholding her salary for 1963-64 and continuing to refuse to reemploy her....

In the Clarendon County case the school district paid salary supplements to white teachers. We are seeking to enjoin the payment of unequal salary based upon race in the school district. The school board has passed a resolution that hereafter supplementary payments would be paid on the basis of the NTE. All the white teachers receive supplements. Many Negro teachers do not.

We are concerned about NTE scores. We have shifted emphasis and will contend that the NTE score is not a proper basis for determining salary. South Carolina is the only state doing this. Most use it to determine whether or not a person is employed. South Carolina decided to use it after Negroes won the equal salary cases. We will be pioneering in this. The case of Mrs. Woods of Allendale has to do with the NTE. Mrs. Woods retook the examination several times in an effort to improve her score. She was accused of receiving aid when her score improved about 200 points or more above the previous score. A relative was accused of aiding her. She did agree to forego the new score in a hearing before the school board. Your executive committee has asked me to go forward with this case.

In the case of Mr. J. C. Prioleau, Jr., of Sumter, the superintendent considered him to be a nonconformist and his contract was not renewed. I have been requested to proceed with this case.[23]

The balance in the PEA Defense Welfare Fund as of February 28, 1967, was $49,400.85. The future use of this fund after the merger was a source of very serious concern to the entire membership of the Association. This particular fund had no counterpart in the SCEA, and the PEA members were strongly opposed to any liquidation of assets which would involve this fund. Not only did they want the fund to remain intact, but they wanted it to be used for the same purpose for which it was established. The Merger Committee was aware of this grave concern of the PEA and made a special provision for it to remain in a separate account to be used for the purpose for which it was originally designed.

After Merger—What?

It is by education I learn to do by choice what other men do by the constraint of fear.

Aristotle

On April 1, 1967, the House of Delegates of the Palmetto Education Association adopted the proposed plan for merger with the South Carolina Education Association after it was revised to include seven additional provisions. A detailed description of this plan and the work of the joint committees may be found in Chapter VII. This concluding chapter focuses upon the activities and operations of the newly organized South Carolina Education Association (SCEA), during the nine years after the merger. An attempt will be made to provide some answers to the following questions:

1. Was the merger agreement fully implemented?

2. To what extent did the components of SCEA (the county associations, departments, committees, etc.) become integrated?

3. Were opportunities for continuous professional growth provided?

4. Did the merger add strength to the legislative program?

5. What effect, if any, did the merger have on services to members?

Information concerning these issues was obtained from a questionnaire that was sent to members of the PEA History Committee and other individuals suggested by the committee who are familiar with the merger plan and have been active in the SCEA since the two organizations merged, in-depth interviews with some of these members, publications of the SCEA, and NEA Merger Evaluations.

IMPLEMENTING THE MERGER AGREEMENT

One of the most significant provisions of the proposed plan for unification of SCEA and PEA was the adoption of a new constitution acceptable to both organizations. A joint committee of four members from each organization, the president of SCEA serving as chairperson, prepared this document; it was ratified by the policy-making bodies of both associations (PEA House of Delegates and SCEA Council of Delegates) during the interim period from April 1, 1967 to April 1, 1968. The adoption of this constitution was of major importance to the new organization, but it was even more significant for the former PEA members because they wanted some assurance that they would have a strong voice in the governance of the new organization. They realized that they could be outvoted since they constituted about one-third of the total membership of the new organization.

During the interim period each association collaborated as equals with the executive committees of both associations meeting together to implement the merger. However, this arrangement was scheduled to last only one year unless for some reason the new constitution was not ratified in which case the interim period would be extended. However, the PEA members were very much concerned about their status after this temporary period came to an end. They would no longer have the "protection" provided by the special provisions of the interim period. Hence, this new instrument of governance had to provide the necessary safeguards for their influence to be effective. The framers of this constitution modified the original merger agreement to provide the following minimal minority guarantees:

1. The Executive Committee shall have nine members with at least two from the former PEA. This provision covered a nine-year period.

2. The Board of Directors shall have nine at-large members with six from the former SCEA and three from the former PEA (until 1977).

3. The Delegate Assembly shall include as voting members past presidents of the former PEA, SCEA, and the merged SCEA.

These constitutional provisions did not give the former PEA members the safeguards they were seeking. Consequently, this document was revised in 1971, 1972, and in 1975. The present constitution and by-laws contain more protective provisions for ethnic minorities. Article V, Section 2 of the constitution published in the *Handbook of 1975–76* states:

> Members from ethnic-minorities shall be represented on the Board (Board of Directors) at least proportionate to the number of active members. If the percentage of ethnic-minority representation fails to achieve proportionate representation, the Delegate Assembly, immediately following the election shall elect at large the number required to assure such representation. Candidates for these positions shall be nominated by open nomination by the ethnic minority delegates at the Assembly and elected by secret ballot by all the delegates. There shall be no more than one ethnic-minority at large director from the same district.[1]

Article IV, Section 5 contains "an ethnic-minority guarantee" which states "If after three (3) years upon adoption, no member of an ethnic-minority has been elected President, nominations shall be restricted to members of such groups."[2]

In addition to these constitutional provisions the executive director of the SCEA sends a memorandum annually to all county presidents informing them of the percentage of ethnic minority membership in each county and the number of ethnic minority delegates it should elect to the Delegate Assembly. In 1975–76 the total number of delegates to be elected from the counties was 226. Of this number, 83 were ethnic minority delegates. Only three counties did not qualify for ethnic minority delegates in 1975–76. They were Oconee, Pickens, and Saluda counties. The constitution states that the allocation of delegates "be based on the ratio of 1:100 active Association members or major fraction there of. Each local affiliate shall be entitled to at least one delegate."[3]

Constitutionally it appears that there are ample safeguards to assure the 8,300 black teachers an effective voice in the governance.

In addition to 83 of the 226 delegates to the Delegate Assembly elected in 1975–76 representing an ethnic minority, there were four black members serving on a nine-member executive committee. They were Mrs. Anna T. Mims, Mrs. Ethel Cooper, Tyrone Gilmore, and Edward E. Taylor. The revised constitution states that "members from ethnic minorities shall be at least proportionate to their membership."[4]

Twelve of the forty-eight members of the Board of Directors that year were Blacks. Two NEA directors, one of whom is Black, also served on the 1976–77 SCEA Board of Directors.

It is also very significant that two former members of the PEA were elected to the presidency of the SCEA within a period of eight years. Mrs. Agnes H. Wilson, the first black educator to serve in this capacity, was elected in 1973–74, and two years later (1975–76), Edward E. Taylor was elevated to the presidency.

Other black members who have held important positions in the SCEA are Clarence Watkins, who served on the Board of Directors from 1968 to 1970 and as an NEA director from 1970 to 1976, and Hudson Barksdale, who also served on the board from 1968 to 1974. John R. Harper and Tyrone Gilmore are also former board members. The members on the 1976–77 Board of Directors representing an ethnic minority are Mrs. Ethel Cooper (one of the NEA directors), Mrs. Anna T. Mims, Mrs. Helen Anderson, Mrs. Agnes H. Wilson, Edward E. Taylor, Mrs. Eloise H. Pearson, William McBride, Mrs. Willie Odell Haynes, Joseph Vaughn, Mrs. Adell Adams, Vandell Davis, Mrs. Rosella Toney, James Tanner, Mrs. Mildred Brevard, and Mrs. Arabella Rich.

Implementing the constitutional phase of the original merger plan has been a long and sometimes difficult procedure. However, it is important to remember as was pointed out in the NEA Merger Evaluation of the SCEA in April 1974:

> . . . the NEA affiliates in S. C. were among the first to prepare for and complete organizational merger. As such they had no pattern to follow; the NEA Merger Guidelines document, as stated earlier, was not issued until six months after the new SCEA constitution had been adopted and the merger completed. Nor did the former PEA and SCEA leaders have the opportunity to learn from the mistakes of other associations. Their mistakes have, in fact, provided object lessons (and resultant safeguards) for the black associations that have participated on merger negotiations in later years.[5]

Considering these negotiation difficulties and the dissatisfaction of most of the six committee members of the PEA with the merger agreement, it is remarkable that the revised constitution brought about as much unity and cooperation as it did. The level of participation is illustrated by the following survey prepared by the Evaluation Committee of NEA which shows the number of Blacks compared to white members who were active in the SCEA from 1968 to 1974.

SURVEY OF NUMBER OF BLACKS AND WHITES ACTIVE IN SCEA, 1968-74

	1968-69		1969-70		1970-71		1971-72		1972-73		1973-74	
	B	W	B	W	B	W	B	W	B	W	B	W
Executive Committee	2	6	2	6	2	6	3	5	3	6	3	6
Board of Directors	10	30	7	27	9	35	9	.29	10	30	13	29
Commissions	24	39	21	42	24	39	30	36	24	39	31	32
Committees	24	34	26	44	33	53	36	47	34	45	30	54
County Presidents	23	45	20	26	21	25	14	32	22	24	17	29
Totals	83	154	76	145	89	158	92	149	93	144	94	150

CHART 5.

The Evaluation Committee of the NEA also made this statement about minority guarantees:

> The concept of racial quotas and minority guarantees is repugnant to many citizens, blacks as well as whites. But as long as our society is one in which the processes of democracy and justice can be subverted by racial discrimination, they will be necessary. And until we are able to eradicate, finally, the blight of bigotry, the professional needs and interests of black educators will continue to be special—urgently requiring the special attention of their association.[6]

Another provision of the merger agreement was the guarantee that all staff of the PEA would be employed with no reduction in salary with continuous employment on the same basis as other regular employees of the new association. It was further agreed that Dr. Walker Solomon, the former PEA executive secretary, would serve as associate executive secretary for special services. As the NEA Evaluation Committee stated, "the title 'associate' clearly implied that Dr. Solomon would be second in rank and salary only to Dr. Gibbons (the executive secretary of the SCEA); and this was the understanding of the PEA merger team. But this is not what happened."[7]

The SCEA employed an assistant executive secretary in 1967 who was given a higher salary and a higher position on the organizational chart than Dr. Solomon. After a protest was made, Dr. Solomon was given a higher salary and was formally named the second-ranking staff official.

This is another example of the weaknesses of the merger agreement. There was at that time no job description for the associate executive secretary for special services, and his relationship to the executive secretary and the assistant executive secretary was not described. Neither was there any provision for Dr. Solomon to succeed Dr. Gibbons if and when Dr. Gibbons decided to leave. The absence of this second provision created another staff problem when Dr. Gibbons resigned on April 14, 1973. The Board of Directors named Dr. Solomon acting executive secretary and directed the Executive Committee to search for a new executive secretary. After interviewing 25 candidates, one of which was Dr. Solomon, the committee presented two names. After the appointment was declined by Dr. Claude Kitchens, the screening committee was directed to reopen its search and present five applicants to the Board.

In the meantime 33 members of the SCEA signed a petition urging that Dr. Solomon be elected to the position of executive secretary and sent copies of the petition to the president and president-elect of the SCEA.

On September 8, 1973, the SCEA Board met again for the purpose of electing a new executive secretary. Dr. Solomon was one of the five applicants presented. The voting was done by secret ballot. Two names were eliminated on the first ballot—one of these was Dr. Solomon's.

There was a protest by the black leaders, and on October 1, 1973 at a meeting of the Southeast Advisory Council, a resolution was adopted requesting the NEA to investigate the matter. Because there was no evidence of deficiencies in Dr. Solomon's performance and after his 24 years of service as PEA executive secretary and SCEA associate executive secretary for special services, and acting executive secretary, it was the feeling of Dr. Solomon's supporters that he deserved the position, especially since this was the second time he was by-passed. While this second incident did not reflect any "breach of contract" in the original plan, it did reveal the consequence of failing to secure safeguards and the reluctance of the Board of Directors at that time to place a black man in such a responsible position.

Staffing the new organization in other areas proceeded without any major complaints. Two staff members, Mrs. Daisy Johnson and Frazier Davis, resigned during the interim period to accept other positions. However, they could have remained on the SCEA staff had they desired to do so.

The 1976–77 SCEA staff consists of 44 persons. Of this number, 24 are professionals and 20 are secretaries, clerks, custodians, etc. Blacks constitute 36 percent of the staff which consists of 8 black professionals and 8 black non-professionals for a total of 16 in the full staff of 44.

Ten of the twenty-four professional staff are local "UniServ" representatives, and in 1975–76 four of them were Blacks. They were Jessie H. Chandler, Kay Patterson, Ruth Williams, and Frank Gilbert. The 1975–65 *Handbook* describes UniServ as follows:

UniServ provides professional staff to local education associations. Through the UniServ program services of the United Teaching Profession become more broadly and equitably available. Educators in small associations as well as their colleagues in larger locals, receive the same professional services. UniServ provides on-the-scene assistance—assistance with educator defense, assistance with better public relations for educators, assistance with the improvement of instruction, and assistance with achieving higher status for the entire profession.[8]

Protection of the Defense Welfare Fund was another provision of the proposed merger which received paramount consideration of the PEA members of the joint committee. Mr. Barksdale, chairman of the PEA Committee on Unification, made a strong case for keeping this fund in a special account and adding to it whenever possible to continue to protect the rights of teachers. The other members of the committee concurred. In keeping with this position of the committee it was agreed by both organizations that the Defense Welfare

Fund be safeguarded, increased, and limited to the protection of teachers.

At the time of merger in 1967 the PEA Defense Welfare Fund was $49,400.85. It eventually was increased to $100,000 and became the responsibility of the Professional Rights and Responsibilities Committee. This committee reviews "a member's request for legal aid when the member's professional and/or legal rights have been violated."[9] The work of this committee is considered so important that the constitution makes a special provision for its composition. Article VII, Section 1 states "Ethnic minority representation on each committee shall be at least proportionate to the membership with the exception of the PR&R Committee which shall be comprised of 50 percent ethnic-minority representation with the exception of the chairperson."[10]

It is significant to note that the first person to use this fund after the merger was a white teacher in Walterboro, South Carolina who objected to being moved from elementary to high school. Prior to merger almost all of the teachers who sought assistance from the PEA Defense Welfare Fund were victims of racial discrimination resulting from salary inequities, unfair dismissals, and intimidation. It is interesting to note that a white teacher needed protection for a much different reason. According to Dr. Solomon, 384 people have sought help from the PR&R Committee and 60 have been given assistance.

The available evidence seems to indicate that with the execption of staffing, the Unification Plan of SCEA and PEA was implemented in keeping with these major provisions. As one respondent to the questionnaire said, "The letter of the merger agreement was followed somewhat reluctantly at first. In recent years both the letter and the spirit have improved."

INTEGRATING THE COMPONENTS OF THE SCEA

When the Liaison Committee was planning the merger of the two associations, the PEA members of that committee insisted that no attempt be made to unify any segments of either organization until the parent bodies (the state associations) were unified. The purpose of this measure was to prevent the loss of membership in the PEA which would have weakened the "negotiate from strength" stance the committee members had taken. This provision of the original agreement was accepted and carried out, but it delayed the full integration of all of the various units of the SCEA. The merger plan contained some recommendations for local associations. Among them were removing racial restrictions in their membership provisions and setting up joint committees to work toward the merger of local associations.

The merger of county associations was expected within a year after the unification of the state associations. April 1969 was the target date for complete merger by county associations. However, this expectation was not realized as early as the planners had envisioned. It took much longer than a year to merge the two local associations into one organization in each county. Some were more reluctant than others to bring about such a change. By 1975 the two associations in each of the 46 counties were merged. The last two counties to affect this change were York and Calhoun. Both were experiencing some local problems. York County eventually merged, but Calhoun County dissolved the old county associations and organized a new one which teachers from both of the former associations joined. This completed the merger process throughout the state. The next area of concern was how efficiently, effectively, and fairly the merged associations, state and local, would operate.

There are a number of indications that the unified associations have been and still are being administered in a manner acceptable to most of the former members of the dual associations. The constitution of the new state organization adopted some minimum governance standards for the local associations which included a guarantee that ethnic minority representation shall be at least proportionate to its ethnic minority membership. Another protective provision of the constitution is the requirement that the Association take an ethnic census every five years beginning with 1974–75. This information will be used to determine proportionate ethnic representation in the future.

It is also significant that in 1976–77, 20 of the 46 county associations have black presidents. This is more than 43 percent of the total number. Some of these black presidents were elected in counties having a low ethnic minority percentage. Five counties with black presidents have an ethnic minority percentage ranging from 17 percent to 29 percent. This information gives us some indication that voting is based more upon merit than race.

Another indication of the extent of integration is to ascertain how many black members are appointed to standing committees. Reference has already been made to the constitutional guarantees for ethnic minorities on these committees. There are 12 standing committees excluding the budget committee. On these committees 37 black members serve. Five of these committees had black chairpersons in 1975–76. The number of chairpersons changes from year to year, but there is usually a number proportionate to the total ethnic minority representation.

OPPORTUNITIES FOR PROFESSIONAL GROWTH

To effectively evaluate the professional growth of the members of the SCEA, it is necessary to consider the criteria used in making the assessment. If membership in professional organizations and the number of delegates to the NEA convention are used as the criteria, the SCEA would rate high. On the other hand, if this growth is judged by the number of teachers who attend the departmental meetings at the annual convention or by the number of departments sponsored by the Association, the rating would not be quite as high.

Before the PEA merged with the SCEA, it had 31 departments. In 1976–77, the SCEA has 14. An argument could be made that the PEA had too many departments and that the present departments of the SCEA are sufficient to meet the needs of all the teachers who wish to improve their teaching competence. However, it must be recognized that the PEA had a more diversified professional improvement program which was well attended by large numbers of teachers in most of the departments. Perhaps the most logical explanation for the decrease in attendance is that there has recently been a tremendous change in the methods of improving teaching techniques. From 1948 to 1967 the departments of the PEA were one of the main sources of professional improvement. Numerous consultants and resource people were brought to the annual conventions to provide information and expertise. The results of these programs were felt in the districts and the counties and eventually filtered down to the classroom.

Today the school districts are expected to provide meaningful in-service training. "The SCEA has developed a bill requiring and enabling all school districts to provide carefully developed, comprehensive in-service training programs for instructional staff beginning with the 1978–79 school year."[11] Local programs, under this act, would be developed by individual school districts to meet their special needs. However, these programs must be approved by the state Department of Education. If this bill is passed by the legislature, the SCEA will more adequately meet the urgent need for providing the continuing professional growth of its members.

The SCEA Governance Handbook For 1976–77 has changed the names of these teacher groups from departments to non-governance affiliates. Of the 14 departments or affiliates, four have black presidents. They are Mrs. Georgia Elam, Home Economics Department; John A. Dorman, Jr., Guidance and Counseling Department; Leroy Fair, South Carolina Driver and Traffic Safety; and Alvin Rucker, South Carolina Council of Teachers of English.

Affiliating with professional organizations is another way of growing professionally. The SCEA sent 147 delegates to the last NEA convention. Of this number, 47, or 32 percent, were Blacks. Other black teachers attended as visitors. The SCEA also has two NEA directors, and one is a Black. These two directors are Mrs. Ethel T. Cooper and Mrs. Nelle H. Taylor, former members of the Executive Committee.

The most noticeably missing department is the higher education unit which was a significant part of the PEA from its inception. The black colleges were closely identified with the Association and supported its programs in many ways. The first constitution of the PEA provided for this department of higher education, and it remained an integral part of the organization until the two organizations merged.

STRENGTHENING THE LEGISLATIVE PROGRAM

One of the most favorable consequences of the merger of the two state associations was the strength it brought to the legislative program of the new organization. For many years prior to 1967 the executive and legislative committees of the PEA used every means at their command to get legislation which would enable them to achieve the educational goals of the Association. Assistance was sought from the NAACP through court actions (see Chapter VIII).

Conferences were held with community leaders to enlist their cooperation and support in getting favorable legislation passed. Considerable progress resulted from court litigation, but very little was realized from legislative action. The SCEA was having more success with the legislative process, but it too needed more strength. When both associations merged, the SCEA had the added weight of 23,000 teachers rather than 15,000. In numbers there is strength—both associations could speak with one voice. Fortunately, the goals of the SCEA were broad enough to include the more specific goals of the PEA which included a compulsory school attendance law, a kindergarten to twelvth-grade plan, free text books, salary increases, tenure law, teacher retirement, and more clerical assistance. The goals of the SCEA in 1975–76 were as follows:

1. A high standard of professional preparation.

2. Leadership in meeting social issues.

3. The safeguards of human and civil rights of all educators and students.

4. Equal educational opportunity through adequate support of education.

5. Economic security for all educators.

6. An effective, independent organization of united educators.

The SCEA also had the experience, the expertise, and the staff to do the lobbying necessary to influence legislation. The PEA had no staff which could devote full time to this assignment and had little if any political influence.

During the nine years since the merger, the SCEA has increased its lobbying efforts and improved and expanded its legislative programs. The January 17, 1977 issue of *The SCEA Emphasis* explains the association's legislative programs in detail and describes how the legislative team, the lobbyists, and the state house team worked together to get the 1977 legislative program in high gear. It is significant to note that the staff member with much of the responsibility for implementing this ambitious program is a Black. He is Joseph Grant and holds the title of manager of governmental affairs.

The legislative program is evidently getting results. The following statement appeared in a recent SCEA publication:

> The House Ways and Means Committee—motivated by teachers' political clout and a renewed desire to update public education—recommended funds for three items long sought by The SCEA: higher pay for the most experienced teachers, free text books for all grades in school; and the continued use of liquor surtax revenues for school operating expenses.[12]

SERVICES TO MEMBERS

It was in the area of services to its members that the members of the PEA Liaison Committee had most of their concern about merger. They knew that the PEA was rendering some services to its members that the SCEA was not providing. Most of these services were related to teacher welfare and the protection of the rights of Negro teachers, and these were precisely what the PEA representatives did not want their members to lose. The Defense Welfare Fund, referred to earlier in this chapter, provided investigations, legal counsel, and financial assistance to PEA members whose rights had been violated.

There were some other services which the PEA committee members wanted to maintain—the departmental workshops, the seminars on general culture, the special projects, field services, the leadership conferences, the planning conferences, the lay conferences, and the affiliation with other professional organizations.

After getting the assurances mentioned elsewhere in this chapter concerning the Defense Welfare Fund and observing the services the SCEA provided its members which would be available to all after merger, the PEA committee members were more inclined to accept the merger plan. It was unrealistic to expect the PEA membership to receive the services they needed with a staff of six to serve 8,500 members when the SCEA, in 1967–68, had a staff of 25 to serve 16,000. By 1976–77, the SCEA staff increased to 44 to serve its 23,000 members.

It is significant to note that the former members of the PEA supported the new organization with a higher percentage of memberships than the former members of SCEA. In 1966–67, the year before merger, the membership of the PEA was 8,618. When the association merged, approximately 8,100 joined the SCEA. The membership in the SCEA in 1966–67 was 16,258. Immediately following merger the membership declined to approximately 13,900. After the first two years of merger the new association experienced some membership gains. Dr. Solomon reported that the SCEA reached an all-time high in membership in 1974–75. During that year the total membership increased to 23,000. Of this number 8,300 were black members. However, there has been a decline in white membership since that time. Without the increasing support of the black teachers at a time when white teacher support is decreasing, the SCEA would lose some of its strength.

Just as the stream of circumstance created the PEA, it also caused it to change its form. The Association was born as a result of segregation when black educators were excluded from the main stream of education in South Carolina and were forced to create their own professional organizations. After segregated schools were declared unconstitutional by the United States Supreme Court, the PEA formulated a "Statement of Principles" expressing its support of and belief in a desegrated public school system. This document also expressed the Association's strong desire to cooperate with other organizations and agencies to implement plans for universal public education in South Carolina within the framework of the ruling of the United States Supreme Court.

With this strong commitment to democracy, free public education, and equality of opportunity, it was to be expected that the PEA would act in conformity with this commitment. Consequently, when the opportunity came to merge with its white counterpart, it cooperated fully.

Even though the Association did not get all of the provisions of the merger plan the majority of the PEA members of the joint committee wanted, they nevertheless accepted the decision of the majority. As has already been pointed out, the former PEA members gave the new organization their support by joining in large numbers. This was done without the minimal guarantees of minority representation in the governance structure which came later.

These actions of the PEA are convincing evidence that the organization did not die when it was merged. Its influence has now taken another form. The strength of the SCEA in the future will depend in a very large measure upon the support of black teachers. Black members should also continue to be involved in every aspect of the new association's programs from governance to committee assignments. Black leadership must not die either on the local or state levels. The more the black members contribute to the processes of democracy and justice, the stronger the SCEA will become for *all* members. Then it can be stated, as it has been said about a competent teacher, that the Palmetto Education Association "belongs to eternity because where its influence ends is never known."

FOOTNOTES

Prologue

[1] John Furman Thomason. *The Foundations of the Public Schools.* Columbia, 1925. p. 57.

[2] *Ibid.,* p. 24.

[3] Colyer Meriwether. *History of Higher Education in South Carolina.* p. 21.

[4] R. Means Davis, "A Sketch of Education in South Carolina. *Handbook for 1883* ("South Carolina"). p. 448.

[5] Henry T. Thompson. *The Establishment of the Public System of South Carolina.* Columbia, 1927. p. 6.

[6] Meriwether, *op. cit.,* pp. 115–16.

[7] Thompson, *op. cit.,* p. 8.

[8] Asa H. Gordon. *Sketches of Negro Life and History in South Carolina.* Georgia, 1929. pp. 84–85.

[9] Lerone Bennett, Jr. *Before the Mayflower: A History of Black America.* Chicago: Johnson, 1961. p. 198.

[10] *Ibid.*

[11] *Proceedings of the Constitutional Convention of South Carolina,"* 1868. p. 100.

[12] *Ibid.*

[13] "The Revised Statues of the State of South Carolina prepared by Commissioners under an Act of the General Assembly, Approved March 9, 1869 to which is prefixed the Constitution of the United States and the Constitution of South Carolina," Article X, Section 5, p. XLIV.

[14] *Proceedings of the Constitutional Convention of South Carolina,* 1868. p. 706.

[15] Thompson, *op. cit.,* p. 9.

[16] *Ibid.,* p. 14.

[17] *Ibid.,* p. 37.

[18] *Ibid.,* p. 38.

[19] M. F. Whittaker, an address before the Palmetto State Teachers Association, March 21, 1940. *PSTA Bulletin.* April 1941. p. 15.

[20] *Ibid.*

[21] *Ibid.*

[22] *Twenty-second Annual Report of the State Superintendent of Education,* 1890. p. 6.

[23] *Twenty-third Annual Report of the State Superintendent of Education,* 1891. p. 36.

[24] *Ibid.,* p. 11.

[25] *Thirty-first Annual Report of the State Superintendent of Education,* 1899. p. 11.

[26] *Ibid.,* p. 13.

[27] *Ibid.,* pp. 13–14.

[28] *Ibid.,* p. 14.

[29] *Thirty-second Annual Report of the State Superintendent of Education,* 1900. pp. 104–105.

[30] *Ibid.,* p. 105.

[31] *Ibid.,* p. 106.

[32] *Ibid.,* p. 106–107.

[33] *Ibid.,* p. 109.

[34] Fred L. Brownlee. *New Day Ascending.* Boston: Pilgrim Press, 1946. p. 116.

[35] Stephen C. Campbell. *The Influence of Negro Baptists on Secondary Education in South Carolina.* Detroit, 1947. p. 12.

[36] *Ibid.,* p. 30.

Chapter I

[1] *The Fifty-sixth Annual Report of the State Superintendent of Education,* p. 3.

[2] Charles A. Beard and Mary R. Beard. *The Rise of American Civilization.* Revised edition. New York: The Macmillan Company, 1933.

[3] *Souvenir Program, Annual Meeting of the Palmetto State Teachers Association.* March 1948. p. 3.

[4] *PSTA Bulletin,* April 1944.

[5] *Annual Reports of the Columbia City Schools,* p. 12.

[6] *Ibid.,* p. 13.

[7] *Ibid.,* p. 11.

[8] *Ibid.,* p. 11.

[9] *Ibid.,* p. 18.

[10] N. C. Nix. *Tentative History of South Carolina State College.* p. 21.

[11] *The Christian Educator,* November 1913. p. 17.

[12] Nix, *op. cit.,* p. 16.

[13] Nix, *op. cit.,* p. 32.

[14] *PSTA Bulletin,* April 1944. p. 13.

[15] *Souvenir Program, op. cit.*

Chapter II

[1] *Souvenir Program, Annual Meeting of the Palmetto State Teachers Association.* March 1948. p. 3.

[2] *Ibid.,* p. 3.

[3] Guerney Nelson. *History of the Palmetto Education Association.* p. 1.

[4] *Souvenir Program, op. cit.,* p. 3.

[5] *PSTA Bulletin,* March 1922. p. 11.

[6] *Ibid.,* p. 13.

[7] *PSTA Bulletin,* March 1920. p. 4.

[8] *Ibid.,* p. 6.

[9] *Ibid.*

[10] *Ibid.,* p. 99.

[11] *Program of the State Teachers Association,* March 10–12, 1921. pp. 7–8.

[12] *Ibid.,* p. 8.

[13] J. L. Cain, address to teachers, March 1922. *PSTA Bulletin,* March 1922. p. 16.

[14] *Ibid.,* p. 17.

[15] *Ibid.,* p. 19.

[16] *PSTA Bulletin,* April, 1923. pp. 7–8.

[17] *Ibid.,* p. 9.

[18] R. W. Mance, President's Address, March 1923. *PSTA Bulletin,* November 1923. p. 14.

[19] *Ibid.,* p. 7.

[20] *Ibid.,* p. 16.

[21] *Ibid.,* p. 16.

[22] *Ibid.,* p. 13.

[23] *PSTA Bulletin,* March 1931. p. 11.

[24] *PSTA Bulletin,* April 1941. pp. 55–56.

[25] *PSTA Bulletin,* March 1936. p. 8.

[26] *PSTA Bulletin,* March 1937. p. 25.

[27] *PSTA Bulletin,* March 1938. p. 31.

[28] Article V, PSTA Constitution, 1939 revision. *PSTA Bulletin,* March 1940. p. 35.

[29] *PSTA Bulletin,* March 1931. p. 15.

Chapter III

[1] *PSTA Bulletin,* April 1941. p. 3.

[2] *PSTA Bulletin,* April 1943. p. 2.

[3] *PSTA Bulletin,* April 1942. p. 47.

[4] *Ibid.,* p. 45.

[5] *PSTA Bulletin,* April 1944. pp. 35–36.

[6] *PSTA Bulletin,* April 1945. p. 38.

[7] *Ibid.,* p. 39.

[8] *Ibid.*

[9] *Ibid.*

[10] *PSTA Bulletin,* April 1946. p. 30.

[11] *PSTA Bulletin,* April 1942. p. 44.

[12] *PSTA Bulletin,* April 1943. p. 37.
[13] *PSTA Bulletin,* April 1946. p. 31.
[14] *Ibid.*

[23] *PSTA Education News,* May 1948. p. 6.
[24] *PSTA Education News,* May 1949. p. 12.
[25] *Ibid.,* p. 12.

Chapter IV

[1] *PSTA Education News,* May 1949. pp. 1–2.
[2] *PSTA Education News,* March 1947. p. 3.
[3] *Ibid.,* p. 4.
[4] *PSTA Bulletin,* April 1946. p. 30.
[5] *PSTA Education News,* October 1946. p. 3.
[6] *PSTA Education News,* November 1947. p. 1.
[7] *PSTA Education News,* October 1946. p. 5.
[8] *Ibid.*
[9] *PSTA Education News,* January 1947. p. 3.
[10] *Ibid.*
[11] *PSTA Education News,* January 1948. p. 12.
[12] *PSTA Education News,* May 1947. p. 3.
[13] *PSTA Education News,* November 1948. p. 1.
[14] *PSTA Education News,* March 1949. p. 2.
[15] *PSTA Education News,* May 1949. p. 1.
[16] *PSTA Education News,* March 1950. p. 4.
[17] *PSTA Education News,* May 1949. p. 9.
[18] *PSTA Education News,* January 1949. p. 1.
[19] *PSTA Education News,* May 1949. p. 12.
[20] *Ibid.,* p. 12.
[21] *Ibid.,* p. 3.
[22] *PSTA Education News,* March 1950. p. 4.

Chapter V

[1] *PSTA Education News,* March 1949. p. 4.
[2] *PSTA Education News,* November 1950. p. 1.
[3] *PSTA Journal,* January 1951. p. 12.
[4] *Ibid.,* pp. 11–12.
[5] *PEA Journal,* November 1957. p. 10.
[6] *South Carolina Education News,* February 1951. p. 6.
[7] *PSTA Journal,* February 1953. p. 3.
[8] *PEA Journal,* November 1957. p. 10.
[9] *PEA Journal,* January 1955. p. 10.
[10] *PEA Journal,* March 1955. p. 3.
[11] *PEA Journal,* March 1959. p. 3.
[12] *Palmetto Education Handbook,* November 1959. p. 3.

Chapter VI

[1] *PEA Journal,* September 1960. p. 1.
[2] *PEA Educational Goals for South Carolina,* November 1961.
[3] *PEA Journal,* October 1961. p. 3.
[4] *PEA Journal,* December 1962.
[5] *PEA Journal,* March 1965. p. 6.
[6] *PEA Journal,* March 1965. p. 7.

Chapter VII

[1] *PEA Journal*, January 1965. p. 31.
[2] *PEA Journal*, December 1964. pp. 1–4.
[3] *Minutes*, PEA House of Delegates. October 30, 1965.
[4] *PEA Journal*, May 1967. p. 21.
[5] *PEA Minutes*, November 5, 1966.
[6] *PEA Journal*, May 1967. pp. 17–18.
[7] *Ibid.*, p. 19.

Chapter VIII

[1] *PSTA Bulletin*, April 1923. p. 30.
[2] *Ibid.*, p. 29.
[3] *Ibid.*
[4] *PSTA Bulletin*, March 1927. p. 16.
[5] *PSTA Bulletin*, March 1928. p. 10.
[6] *Ibid.*, p. 10.
[7] *PSTA Bulletin*, March 1929. p. 9.
[8] *Ibid.*, p. 11.
[9] *PSTA Bulletin*, March 1931. p. 20.
[10] *Ibid.*, p. 21.
[11] *PSTA Bulletin*, March 1936. p. 18.
[12] *Ibid.*, p. 18.
[13] *Ibid.*, p. 19.
[14] *Ibid.*
[15] *Ibid.*
[16] *PSTA Bulletin*, March 1939. p. 32.
[17] *PEA Journal*, March 1956. p. 3.
[18] *PSTA Bulletin*, April 1942. p. 44.
[19] *Ibid.*, p. 44.
[20] *Ibid.*, p. 45.

[21] *Minutes*, PSTA House of Delegates. November 17, 1951.
[22] *Minutes*, PSTA House of Delegates. March 27, 1952.
[23] *Minutes*, PSTA House of Delegates. March 26, 1953.
[24] PEA Constitution, revised 1957, Article XV. Section 1. *Palmetto Education Association Handbook*. November 1959. p. 12.

Chapter IX

[1] *Souvenir Program, Annual Meeting of the Palmetto State Teachers Association*, March 1948. p. 3.
[2] *PSTA Bulletin*, March 1936. p. 2.
[3] *Ibid.*
[4] *Palmetto Education Association Handbook*, November 1959. p. 24.
[5] *PEA Journal*, November 1956. p. 11.

Chapter X

[1] *PSTA Bulletin*, March 1920. pp. 6–7.
[2] *PSTA Bulletin*, March 1921. p. 5.
[3] *PSTA Bulletin*, March 1922. p. 13.
[4] *PSTA Bulletin*, March 1929. p. 3.
[5] *PSTA Bulletin*, March 1937. p. 5.
[6] *Ibid.*, p. 18.
[7] *PEA Journal*, May 1961. p. 12.
[8] *PEA Journal*, May 1962. p. 13.
[9] *PEA Journal*, May 1963. p. 3.
[10] *Minutes*, PEA House of Delegates. March 4, 1967. p. 7.